Amongst the Ruins

Metier Books

ISBN: 978-1-60594-414-2

Printed in the United States of America by Metier

Library of Congress Control Number: 2010922682

Amongst the Ruins

Once upon a time . . .

During the cold bitter winter month of January, in a public hospital lay a beautiful woman. Her bloodline was African American and Native American. She had sisters and one brother, who un like her, had beautiful, light skin . . . pretty, yet she lived in an era where dark skin was frowned upon.

There she lay, so full of poverty, not only poverty from the lack of material things in life, but poverty that dwelt deep in her soul. Once, at a very early age, under some shack, she had conceived another beautiful child. . . One that she loved with all her heart, but an angry mother said no to the rearing of this beautiful child. The child was torn from her; she was forced to give the child away and her womb closed up so that nothing would live there again, a great part of her heart closed also. What pain! What agony, amidst all else that was happing at that time: racism and hatred for the African American person, no education to be had, and so much pain. For fifteen years, she had been barren; now, there she lay, giving birth for the fourth time. She'd had not much, if any, prenatal care. This wasn't supposed to be.

In the cold month of January in a lonely room in a public hospital where healthcare to African Americans was not good, the woman was almost at the point of hysteria from the prolonged labor pains. After thirty hours, her body now automatically heaved: "Push…Push … Push! But the woman only screamed from pain. Finally, one last time, she gave it all that she had; her womb opened, and just as the child was coming, her womb began to close, almost choking an already half-dead fetus….

And so a child is born. No baby showers, no happy balloons, no one there to support the mother. As the doctor cuts the cord he notices that the child, a breech delivery, is still and blue. He shakes his head. He just looks and lays the child to the side of the mother. Unlike most mothers, she shows no sparkle of joy, no feeling of pride in the birth, only contempt. She doesn't ask how the child is; she simply closes her eyes. The infant is placed on the table and is about to be covered when an old doctor happens by and spots life . . . movement in the infant. Quickly he turns the small, limp body upside down and begins to hit the child. Three or more times he slaps the tiny body, and then blows into its mouth. He uses suction and suddenly a loud scream fills the delivery room. He places the child on the mother's chest, and while she is being cleaned, she finds the strength to lay the child to the side. Days pass and time goes on. How can any good come of this? Even a flower needs water to live, and so a child needs love.

♦♦♦

As I grew, I can recall my surroundings: downstairs in a basement, two rooms next to a funeral home. Down those steps my rights are violated, my rights to life and the pursuit of happiness. I am robbed of a childhood. Follow my story; over time, I will reveal the smell of urine the drunks pissed down the cement stairs, and seeing Miss Viola as Mr. Frank f-----g her like she is a dog. The curtains are always open. Look into the front room. Look at the cracked mirror on the dresser. Look at the bare cement floor. There is a single bed. One window a door frame leads into the next room to the right. Look at the sink: filth, roaches, dirty dishes, and sometimes maggots from where the flies have flown onto the leftover food. There is a bed; three children sleep there with the mother. See the children, as they lie in bed at night, looking and listening to the large black rats fighting over food and territory and sometimes killing each other. The children smell the stench of the rats blood, and during the night, when they have to use the bathroom, they pass by cages of 'possums and different animals that the grocer sells upstairs. No *I love you* or, even *good night*, only screams of a man beating his wife half to death.

♦♦♦

These are my memories from my earliest childhood. We would wear whatever hand-me-downs the Johnsons, her employers, gave Mother; they were the only ones to ever give us toys. On Friday evenings, Daddy would get dressed in his pointy-toed orange Stacy Adams, and after getting a bath from the tin tub, he'd be ready to paint the town, go up on the corner and raise some hell, cut one or two fellows, come home, beat everyone in the house, and take back the few dollars he had given to Mother.

It was commonplace for us kids to drain the milk cartons that had been discarded behind the school, or on a Saturday when the church folks had a bar-be-cue, when no one was looking, we would run by and grab a hot slab from the burning grill, so hungry we were, and then we'd sit on the sidewalk and wait for Momma to get off the bus so we could eat whatever leftovers she had brought us from the Johnson's. I can remember in the first grade going to the Fern Bank Science Center, and the night before, I had eaten a whole pack of Ex-lax, and I can remember crapping all over myself and the other children laughing at me. I cried. The teacher said, "What the hell is wrong with you?" and jerked my arm so hard it went numb. A nice lady saw what was happening and came to help me. The teacher spanked me hard, and they told my sister and she told Momma, and again I was beaten brutally. I used to have severe earaches, and Momma said the reason for that was when I was around three and she had to leave me with my father—we lived in the basement, but there were rooms upstairs—and my father was having an affair with Mrs. Willie Andrews, so he left me on the porch, and I fell from the third floor. Momma said you could not recognize me from the swelling of my head and face. Had anyone cared, someone would have called the police, but when you are African American and poor, who cares? I can remember playing on the street and getting hit by passing cars, yet not being taken to the doctor.

One day, as I played in the back field, which was full of broken glass, I sat on the large brown wooden slabs and I found me a baby doll. I played with it for hours, and when the night came, I went inside carrying my baby doll. My mother screamed and said, "Take that damn thing out of here!" I began to cry because I'd never had a doll. She slapped my face and said, "You stupid f---er, that's a damn real baby! Where did you get it?" And I said, "Outside in the field." I guess someone had a miscarriage or whatever. Then once again, another time, as I was looking in the boxes behind the funeral home, I found another baby in a box with some collard greens.

Sometimes we would smell the bottles that the funeral home used. Later, I learned that it was embalming fluid; it sure was strong to smell. I had a sister, that did not live with us and every now and again, she would contact my mother. She hated my father because of how he treated Mother. Her life was filled with pain, I later learned, because she had been given away as a child. Once, she gave me a pretty blue dress. I remember it, even to this day. I always remember all genuine acts of sincere kindness to me.

One day, when I was in maybe the third or fourth grade and it was my turn to answer the math problem, I wrote the wrong answer, and the children laughed. No one helped me with schoolwork, and I just didn't know. To this day I have problems with math.

We got to go to the Johnsons with mother, because no one would keep us. When we got to the beautiful house, we had to remain in the basement in the wagon that belonged to her child, and we could not make noise, so we were quiet. The love and attention mother provided to the Johnsons produced doctors and lawyers, but her own kids died.

Daddy never had a steady job. Now, this is where the army was sorry as hell. He fought in World War II, and I think he may have suffered from what happened in the war with post-traumatic stress disorder. He often spoke of New Guinea and all the killings he'd witnessed. He would sometimes wake up screaming, "Get the dead man off me!" He sometimes thought we were Japs and would grab one of us and choke us. He didn't have a steady job; he just caught out on the corner and whatever he got, he would drink it up, except a few dollars that he would give to Momma, and then he'd come and take it back. I can remember him beating my brother and me. I would run and crawl under the bed, and he would take that broom and jug under the bed. I would hold onto the iron springs; if I didn't, he would beat me nearly to death. He never explained why. He would beat instead of talk. Momma would be drunk and fry some chicken and burn it bad, and they would make us eat it.

After a while, we had to move to Markham Street, because the health department closed that place where we lived down. Imagine that, after all the agony and abuse. Well, things were worse on Markham Street. There was a hotel called the Markham Street Hotel. Poor families lived there, including us. The place only had one nasty bathroom for everyone, and you had to cut wood for a fire and heat water to bathe. Hell, I don't remember too much bathing, not to mention never having a kitchen table. Hells, for that matter, not even a kitchen.

I began a new school. I was fighting from the first day almost to the last. At the age of seven, I followed my brother and Peewee to Rich's Department Store. I saw so many things, and I was fascinated, so when I saw them steal, I did the same. As I was leaving the store, the detective . . . Booker I later learned was his name . . . he asked if I had something that did not belong to me. I said, "No, sir." He said, "Well, I believe you do," and that time he just took the small radio from my pocket and told me not to do that again. I said "Yes, sir." A few days later, I went back with the boys again, and they showed me how to steal, and that went on for some years.

Momma was drinking more and more. Daddy was mean to us, and Momma had another baby. When she went in the hospital, my father fed us pigeons he caught. Momma came back, only to be beaten like a dog. He stomped her, and she had just had that baby. I waited until he was asleep and went outside and got the brick we kept there to prop the firewood when we cut it. My intention was to drop it in his face, but Momma saw me and screamed, and he woke up. I ran out the door into the night. My sister caught up with me. She thought he had killed me.

Each time he would beat Momma, I would run and get the police, only for her to say everything was fine. By this time, my brother had been placed in a foster home. He kept getting caught stealing, first from Rich's, then Davidson's. Momma cried; she loved him so much.

Let's talk about Momma a little. She was once a pretty woman, from what I can see in this picture, but I could also see that she was always sad, so I asked my aunt a, who is still alive, eighty years old. I asked her questions often about Momma. She said that their mother, whose name was Paralee, was an alcoholic and would abuse them. Back to Momma . . . Her father was an Indian—a Native American—it seems, from what I can pick up. Back in the day, females interacted with different men on various occasions for money, but I am told that Momma was an introverted type and always had a problem with being dark skinned. Back during that time, it was not considered a good thing to be dark. But you must understand, her hair was straight as a board. Why wasn't she considered beautiful? More questions, huh? She was not a very affectionate person . . . well, not to me. She was somewhat kinder to my brothers and my sister, but there again, I was dark. I can remember back when I was very young and my grandmother was still alive. Momma would take us to Grandma's house, and we had to sit on the floor. She would say, "Don't put that black-ass child on my bed." She was never happy to see us. And there was another great mystery to me. I have an older sister, and Mother had to give her away at a very young age, and that, even to this day, is still between us. We will talk more about her.

Back to Momma. . .

I can think back to Mitchell Street. Sometimes we went to school; sometimes we did not. No one seemed to care, not the school, not the parents, not the government, so around the time we knew the bus would come, we would run up to the street—Hunter Street was its name. I was always happy to see Momma. Tears are falling from my eyes. Why? Because I can still so plainly see four small kids who had been left to rear themselves, still feeling happy to see their mother. She would look at us, and we would go back down the stairs and into what was supposed to be a home, hungry, our feet cut from being barefooted. Sometimes my sister would want to go off with other big girls to Ms. Toggle's, or just for a walk. When we went to the store, the man who owned the place would sit behind the register and smoke that cigar and watch, and when his wife wasn't there, he would touch us. My sister was supposed to be taking care of me, but she would be so mean! If she was supposed to comb my hair, she would pull it so hard and plait it so tight my skin would raise up. I had sores from something called impetigo. It's a wonder and an act of God I didn't have everything! I would follow Falinda, and she would hit me and tell me to go home. Once I got hit by a car while I was trying to follow her. What else was strange . . . if someone hit me with a car, they never took me to the hospital. If I could stand . . . then okay. I couldn't tell Momma because I would get a beating.

Sometimes, after my father would come back from being up on Mitchell Street and there was no food left, he would beat Momma so bad! Each time he hit her, I hated him more. I had to leave for a while, mainly to collect myself. Going back inside caused such pain. But back to Momma. I never witnessed her and my father showing any affection toward each other. Did they hate each other? Were they thrown together because of us? So many questions. . .

♦♦♦

I went to school today and received a D on my test. Feeling real *f--ked* up because it means so much for me to succeed at this. I went to my therapist. This was my second visit. I will discuss my sessions later.

But back to my mother. She never really talked to me when I was young. Maybe she would talk to my older sister sometimes. She was never, ever happy.

Now, let's go back to Markham Street Hotel. We lived around back, and to get there, you had to walk through the alleyway full of glass bottles and plenty of huge rats. A fence separated this company's parking lot from our door. I wanted to say front door, but there was only one door and one room. Daddy had his own bed; Momma and the rest of us shared a bed. It was made of iron with iron springs and a regular feather mattress. There again, we would lie and watch the rats fight, not over food, but just fight. Joe Shaffer, a Jew, owned this piece of shit, and had the heart to allow children to live there. Why was life so damn hard and unfair? I often wondered, was my family under some curse? As this tragedy unfolds, you will see why I ask, and why I felt this way on Markham Street.

One day, Dr. Martin Luther King, Jr. and some more men came by, and I saw tears well up in his eyes, and he said. "My God . . . Oh, my God." He came over to me and he put his arm around me, and I saw him turn and wipe a tear away. He said, "What's your name?" and I told him. I also told him I was hungry and he instructed the other man to give us some Kentucky Fried Chicken. He must have known that we would be without food. We were so hungry! We said "thank you," and he said that things would get better by and by.

In the System . . .

This is where my life with the juvenile justice system started. I went back uptown and began to steal. First, my sister would tell me to bring her a pretty doll, so I would go and steal a doll. Back on Mitchell Street, if the other girls would fight my sister, I would jump in. I could fight like a boy, so I did a pretty good job of protecting her. My father was bad about cutting people with his knife, so I watched, and I became pretty good with a knife myself. One time I got into a fight with a girl because she was getting the best of my sister. She was bigger than both of us. I got my queen blade out and began to stab her. That got her off of us, but her mother had me sent to Juvenile Hall, and that's when it began. I was seven years old. Stealing was my first record, then fighting. I was labeled ungovernable. Later, after so many incidents, I was sent to a youth development center.

But let's go back awhile . . . to an episode of molestation that happened to me at the age of nine. We were living on Markham Street, and I had met this lady who lived in the neighborhood. She was nice; she gave me baths and a nice clean place to rest when I would come over and spend the night. Her husband was a mover, and sometimes he went out of town, so she would ask me to spend the night. I always slept on the rollaway bed. She lived next to a building that had a tin roof. So this one night, as the rain fell hard on the roof and the lighting flashed across the sky, she told me to come and share her bed, so I did. As I lay there, her hand moved slowly across my little body, and I was not afraid because she had hugged me often, rubbing my legs and across my chest. I could tell that this was different from before. She continued rubbing and she touched my privates. I jumped, because no one ever touched me there. She held me closer and whispered, "I am not going to hurt you." The rain was hard and so was my breathing. She placed her mouth on my jaw and softly kissed it saying, "It's all right," then she pushed my legs apart and touched me again. I started to cry; she was scaring me. But she continued to say, "It's all right." She opened my legs wider and got between them and began to lick my face. Then she kissed my lips and went on down my body, and when she tried to put her mouth on me, I said no, but she was stronger than I was. As she continued, I began to shake. She scared me so bad! She stopped and crawled up beside me and said, "Please just relax." I was shaking so bad I almost peed in her bed. She made me promise not to tell. I said ok. Hell, I did not understand what she was doing, so I did not tell, but like many other things that grown people did, I did not like or understand it. How is it that a child should have to endure so much? Where is God when a child is losing her innocence, and in the process, a monster is being created out of something inherently beautiful?

I found out a little more about my mother and how she met my father. I was told that she had very high hopes when she met him. He was in the service and had the air of hope. I can imagine that back during that time, given the life she lived, a nice man would be like a breath of fresh air. I had sisters, and each one of them had a different father, but from what I can gather, I was a dark one, and so he never wanted to accept me. Mother had a dark boyfriend before him, and maybe he had thoughts that I wasn't his. Maybe that's one of the many reasons he would beat me almost every day.

♦♦♦

Every time I write in this soon-to-be bestseller, it rips my soul, and it takes me a few days to recover. I was in the shower and this book came into full play in my head. Now, it's not for money that I am doing this, but mainly it's for my three children who hate the ground that I walk on. Just stay with the road that leads to the jewels amongst the ruins and feel free to rake through my life. And if there is help for anyone who may have trodden the same path or a similar one, use my life to redesign yours, because I am learning that life goes on. The reason it has taken so long to write this is that I really don't know if anyone would read it, but my heart insists that I do it.

I climbed back up the tree next to the place I lived. (I did not mention that I loved to climb trees.) I climbed a very high one today. This was the day after that awful night at my neighbor's. I wondered why Mrs. Mickey had done that to me. I cried and looked at the beauty of the sky—no rats, no fighting, and no cursing no violations —just beauty. If you will notice, I don't talk much about school. I didn't go very much, and trust me; I can feel the pain of that to this very day as I struggle to type this manuscript. I often ask why, now that today everyone claims to be interested in the success of youth. I wished all my life that someone would have seen past my acts that caused pain and reached out to help me. Even today, with all the so-called help, there is another Eloise who is not getting any. Do you wonder why I chose the title *Jewels Amongst the Ruins*? Well, in every human, I believe there is a jewel of a person, but circumstances cause that jewel to get misplaced and the shine dulls, until it is rediscovered. But look at the lost time. We both know the two things that can never be replaced are innocence and time. If you are reading this book now, you are still in the beginning, but if you have a child, just look at him or her and evaluate whether are you giving that child a chance at life. Are you rearing that child to be a productive human or a monster? Only you know the truth, and of course, God knows. How could you not love that which, in making love, the two of you created? And it was intentional, because you didn't use protection, unless it was conceived of ill-gotten ways, and if so my heart bleeds for both of you. This is to the real smart leaders of the world: If only you would stop and evaluate the process of governing people and stop writing lies, and actually develop a system that interacts with the people! Because everyone who falls through the holes will resurface and more than likely cause pain to innocent people, out of their own pain. We all know by now that people are the same as far as their need to be loved, needed, appreciated, and respected. And every child deserves a healthy start. When I look back on my life, I see that I've been like someone reared in the wilderness. As someone told me, I raised myself. Now, that's not right. I was never taught right from wrong, but this world held me accountable. And to those of you, who are reading this, know that the world will hold you accountable.

After so many trips to the juvenile facility, finally, a judge said that it was enough, and to remove this child and place her in foster care. This was before the trip to the youth development center. I can remember my days as a child in Juvenile Hall. The ladies who worked there were kind. I can't write their names; I don't have permission. But I remember them. I was only seven years old and could not reach the hole in the door in the Juvenile Hall; I was too short. But there I could shower, and there I began to develop into the monster I became.

Back to the foster home . . .

I was placed with a family that was supposed to be holy and have my best interests at heart. But the woman constantly reminded me of how sinful I was, and her husband would try to rape me in the garage. One day he almost succeeded. This happened while we lived on Markham Street in the hotel. The time he almost did it, I was cutting their grass, and I had to go into the shed. There he was, dick in hand, waving for me to come closer. I grabbed this thing that was made like a round blade and I held it and told him that I would cut that dick of his off if he came any closer. I backed out of the shed and began to run up the road, and I did not stop until I came to the main road. I walked until I saw a bus and begged the man to take me home, back to Markham Street. My mother was angry to see me, but strange as it may seem, I was happy to see her. She said I could not stay there, so I slept under a bridge and went back to her house the next day, only to be picked up by the police and taken back to the Juvenile Hall. This time, I was placed in the Carrie Steel Pitts Orphan Home. There were plenty of children there, and I liked it because after I had been there a while, I saw my brother. This made me happy, because I had missed him, and I really didn't understand where he had gone. We said hello and we cried. I lived in Cottage Seven where the young people lived. After a while, I was returned home, only to get into more trouble. I stabbed a girl for beating my sister. This time I was on my way to the youth development center in Augusta, Georgia. I can remember riding up in a van. There were others in the van, but I was so very afraid. We were told to get off and come inside. As we walked into this building, I could see girls looking at us through windows. We were each assigned a building. There were older girls who were house monitors over us younger ones. Right away, a girl named Shirley pointed to me and said for me to bring my belongings to her room. The rooms only had a curtain for a door. Only God knows what she had me doing behind that curtain—from washing her clothes to making her life more pleasant. One day she went too far: she told me to go down on her, and she meant right then and there. I said, “You are on your period.” The reason I knew was I washed her panties. She slapped me and said, “Bitch, don’t you ever talk back to me or say no.” I then said, “I don’t give a f—k what you say; I am not going to lick your bloody ass.” I may have been afraid of her because she was so much bigger than me, but it only reminded me of a time when my sister was beating the hell out of me for no reason . . . oh, because my mother told her to comb my hair. Anyway, I couldn’t whip her, so I did the next best thing: I got the frying pan and knocked the hell out of her. You can bet that stopped her from beating me. But this was a different case. This girl was getting the best of me. I ran down the hall, through the dining room, and into the kitchen. I grabbed a can-opener, the kind that you pull up from the table, turned around, and hit that bitch right in the face. Blood flew everywhere, and I was placed in the hole for almost a year—not just for hitting her, but for escaping while in lockdown. I was there because I defended myself. While I was there, I was sitting looking out through the bars, and I saw my sister Linda as she was leaving the facility. I got mad because they would not allow her to see me, so that night, I and others who were in the hole kicked the window out and escaped. They always told us the place was surrounded by quicksand, which was a lie. They just didn't want us to try to run away. There was a huge floodlight that illuminated the entire place, but we got past the lighted area. I tell you, we had balls of steel! The reason I say that is it was so dark and the woods were thick, but we braved it and walked up a long, dark street for what seemed like miles. Finally, we spotted a service station. We had no money, so we had little choice but to steal. As we left and got back on the highway, we got a ride. Whew . . . I was happy, but not for long. The driver took us straight back to the place. All that walking for nothing! Another twelve months added to my sentence.

Finally, the day came when I was old enough to get out, and I went back to Atlanta. I had left as a girl, and I came back an angry woman.

The first place I went was to Mickey.

For so many years, she had taken advantage of me. After being in the room with this other bitch, I now understood what Mickey had done to me—a grown woman molesting little girls. I went to her house and she seemed to be happy to see me. She tried to hug me, and I beat the crap out of her. I started to cut her throat, but I thought better of it. As I stomped her, I cried, "Why?" But I knew the answer: It was because she knew how bad my life was. And she only added to my problems in a very profound way. I then went to find my mother. She still hated the sight of me, but she let me stay with her.

Hippie Days . . .

Now we are going to visit my hippie days. One day, while we were in Piedmont Park, I met some members of the Hell's Angels. This was a group of bikers, and I loved to hang around them. One night, we went to Lake Lanier, and everybody got naked and went swimming. Everything was fine at first, until something happened between a couple of dudes and the bikers got together and beat one dude beyond life and then pissed on him. They told us to leave, but as we were leaving, I heard a horrible scream and a loud shot. We got the hell out of there. Rumor had it, they cut his nuts off. I'm not sure why.

Then began the road to the point of no return. We had moved to Abbott Street in the Harris Homes. We ended up there because we had been put out of our room on Markham Street. Eight dollars a week, and we got put out of the Markham Hotel. God works in truly mysterious ways! No more Daddy! Great! We were placed in foster care . . . . No, it was the shelter with the juvenile authorities. One of my brothers, the younger one, ran away. I caught him on the bridge, and we went back to our new home: no furniture cardboard boxes for beds, and no food, but we were together and enrolled in a new school. A little time passed, and damn! I came home one day, and there sat Daddy with a mangy black dog named Midnight. I liked it.

I would watch my mother sit on the floor and scratch her legs until they would bleed. Then the drinking began, and the life of crime. First, it was burglary. That went on for some time. Once I went in to this African's house. The only way you could get in was to climb the front door and up through the transom. As I got in and was trying to open the front door to let my buddies in, the owner came out of a room with a very long gun, and I almost fainted from fear. He said, "Open the door." I was happy because together we were strong as hell. He was close behind me, and I swung the door open hard and it hit him in the face. The others came in, but he was quick, and he was right back on his feet, gun in hand. He talked to us and called the law. They locked us up, but because it was our first time, they were not hard on us. That was my first visit to jail, and it did not scare me.

I did more break-ins, and now I had my own gun. We would go to the clubs and dance and fight, and go to the mall and steal outfits. By now, we were stealing from different stores. When I brought someone to the house, my mother would curse them out. She dipped snuff, and she would spit on my friends. I was so embarrassed by her actions! She often pointed her finger at me and would say "Black dike bitch, you are going to have a hard life." She and Daddy were drinking like a couple of fish and making life unbearable, so I roamed the street by night and slept by day. I met all types of pimps and hoes, and I became a creature of the night.

My rage inside was growing out of control. More stealing and hanging out at night by now. My girl friends and I were out there, and we were having a ripping good time. I already knew Tony Sr.. I was at this big house where one of my friends lived with a lady who would take people in. Everyone hung out there. Momma would go to this same street to get liquor. One day I saw Tony sr there, sleeping on the sofa, and I couldn't resist kissing him. I did and hid. He opened his eyes and went right back to sleep. I stared at him. He was the first dude I had ever made love to. He was very nice and gentle. He played basketball. His mother didn't care much for me because I had a reputation, and she, being the good mother, wanted more for her son.

♦♦♦

Momma told me not to get in people's cars. One day, I was walking to the store to get some washing detergent for Momma. I had on a halter and jeans shorts. Ashby Street was very busy, and as I walked up the street, this youngish man in a green hatchback Mustang drove by very slowly. He said, "Can I give you a lift?" I said, "Naw, that's okay." He insisted, so I gave in and got in the car. He took me to the store and then he said, "I will take you back home." I said okay, and when we left the store, he got onto the Interstate. "Where are you going," I asked him, and he said, "I have just got to go to the next exit to pick up something." I said all right and he drove to the next exit, and then he turned into this empty church parking lot. I said again, "Where are you going?" He said he was taking a shortcut, and he pulled into a dark spot and stopped the car. Right away, he hit me in my face so hard my nose bled, and he started to tear at my clothes. I managed to say, "OK, just let me pee." He pushed me out of the car, holding my hair. I broke away and began to run. He outran me and dragged me back to the car and hit me in the head. He said, "Bitch, if you want to live, don't try anything stupid." He ripped all my clothes off and pried my legs apart and merciless raped me. He was so huge he tore my body apart. After he'd finished, he told me to kiss him. Then he kicked me out of the car and left me lying naked in the dirt. No one except someone that this has happened to can understand the filth . . . how nasty you feel . . . and the shame. He hurt much more than my body; he hurt my psyche and tortured my soul. I managed to walk to the street, where I passed out. When I came to, I saw a man taking his coat off. I screamed. I thought he was going to rape me too. But he was covering me up. He took me to the police and they hurried and took me to the hospital. I received eleven stitches and told my story. Someone came to pick me up and take me home. When my mother found out what had happened, she said he should have killed me.

We lived in Harris Homes. There were nice people who lived in those apartments. The apartments were nice because white people had lived there first and they kept them up. So different from what I had been exposed to early on in life! As I look back, I cannot believe that I went through all I did and survived. I started breaking in people's apartments and really hanging in the streets. Angry, frustrated, ignorant, misused, abused, and dangerous. There was a lady who lived a couple doors up from us who had two sons and two daughters. She did not allow her children to associate with me because I was bad, but she would come and care for my parents at night.

I would go to the A&P food store and steal food. Once this man caught me, and I guess he felt sorry for me. He let me go and I wore it out. I kept going back, so finally he asked me why I did that. "To eat," I told him. And where did I live? he wanted to know. I told him I had a sister I bet he would like to meet. By now, my sister had a baby, but she didn't stop going to school. She went to night school and worked for Internal Revenue Service and was voted most likely to succeed. But that story will take a different turn.

Before I go into another part of the story, let's talk about the effects of adolescence. First off, the true measure of this time of life is seldom discussed in enough depth. It is a very trying time in a person's life that no one seems to know exactly how to explain. I do know that it's either like changing into The Hulk or into a beautiful person. For me it was the beast. It is often taken so lightly . . . being a teenager . . . because for some reason, unknown to most, that transition shows what your childhood was, and determines what your adult life will be for many years. Well, it was like that for me, anyway. No two people are the same, yet sometimes the same thing might happen to two people at different times. Like when I was raped. That was a life-shaping event and it felt the same when I was a child. Now that I look back, how could I have been much different? My life from birth was the perfect storm: walls of million-foot-high waves all around me, and I was never taught to swim. If you cannot swim, you sink. But not only do you sink yourself, you will cause countless others to sink with you from your random acts, sometimes reaching out sometimes lashing out. I never meant to hurt anyone, but my life was twenty-four/seven pain. There were times when I was young and adults knew that I was headed the wrong way but they only saw the wrong that I was doing. Instead of talking and pointing fingers, maybe if they had reached out more . . .well, who knows? There was a time I heard that blacks would care for each other's children and try to be the parent they knew the child never had. I must have come along at the wrong time, or maybe I was such a menace they feared me. But that has a bad ring to it . . . afraid of a child living in government homes, where everyone knows everyone and everything about you. Being poor makes the whole community family, like it or not. It was so wrong of me to disrespect my mother as I did, but it was also wrong for her to allow my father to disrespect her in my face. I know the key word is respect. *Honor* thy mother and father. It would have been hard for me to honor anyone in my youth; I was too busy trying to survive. In my head, there was this highway, and it had so many roads and intersections. I traveled them all at one time or another. How could I have shown love? I had never known it. How could I have loved and respected God? I was never taught how. I am not looking for excuses or placing blame. I am just telling the story the way it happened. Yesterday I looked at my mother's picture on the wall, and I thought, *what* in the world happened? *Who* are *you?* Who am I? I realized I had begun to build a very thick maze, and I placed myself in the middle of it for protection. Now, animals are born with the sense to protect themselves. Animals, right? That's what I was, a human animal. Today, I can't believe who, how, why, and all of the above when I hear people talk about being gangster, as if that's the thing to be. But back then, that was all I ever knew.

♦♦♦

I can remember this young girl—myself—not knowing about periods, and when mine started, it scared the crap out of me. I tore up an old sheet and put it on. A stranger told me what it was. This world has become so desensitized to human pain that we look for ways to rid ourselves of caring, when really, if you consider it, looking the other way, locking people away only creates more chaos. As I look back to Harris Homes and I look deeper, I can see why the adults kept their distance. Each time the police came and got me, they would be sitting on their porches watching. After a while, they'd shake their heads and say, "That Eloise . . . ." They had become okay with it, because they knew what I did to the community, and perhaps they thought I deserved it.

Let's talk about living with an alcoholic. That's another subject that is thought of less than it should be. No child should ever have to endure an adult's sickness, and there again, just like everyone knows the bad kid, so do they know the alcoholic. Now, tell me this. How in the hell did it become okay to sell poison? Everyone knows the effects of it, just like street drugs, but it's all about the money. Who cares about a child having to live being cursed every day of her life, spit on and beaten and raped and only God knows what else they must endure. It's all about the money. I had a friend, and every time her father would get drunk, he would find his way to her and rape her. She never told anyone, but she hated men. Now, given a different set of circumstances, she might be happily married with kids and not be gay. Yes, we have every kind of government system in place, and no one gives a stiff fuck. It's all paperwork and procedure. No one cares about the reason why we can't just move on. Can't we see what's going on? I hear daily that you can't live in the past. Now please, for once be honest. You know that if you don't put closure to tragedies in your life, it's an ongoing situation. I have a wounded soul and every day I try to live a normal life. Some people just sum it up that people like me are insane, depressed, or any other label they can come up with. But for me, it was a broken heart and a wounded soul. Man, if he can't understand something, will give it a name and reason, even if it's wrong. That's just due process. Alcohol violates the Constitution. Tell me, how can you pursue life, liberty, and happiness drunk? Not only does it kill you physically, it kills mentally. It kills the one who drinks, and it kills the one who has to live with the one who drinks. There again, we have become accepting of the entire process, yet we complain about the outcome. Everything that we do or say speaks volumes about the person inside looking out. Our eyes reveal the very essence of who we are, for real. Have you ever wondered when you look in the mirror, who am I? Not what role in life you play, but who you really are. I have learned how to talk and walk so that I can be accepted, but it doesn't give me peace. I know there is no magic answer and what is done is done. Writing this book gives me the privilege to say that there are always two sides to every story. I can tell my side. Perhaps getting it out will grant me peace before I die. And I hope it will explain some things to the many people I love and was not able to tell, especially three in particular. Inside, there is a little girl always looking at me, and she cries out, *why* wasn't I protected and given a chance? Why wasn't I lovable*? What's* wrong with me*?* I live way deep inside. Perhaps this may sound odd, when I say inside of me lives a little girl who is lodged in my soul and all day and night, and even in my sleep, she cries. I can remember back as when I was a child, my brother, whom I still love, was arrested for the murder of a white woman who was stabbed over two hundred times. One night the police came to my apartment in the Harris Homes with a search warrant. My mother let them in, and they went to his room and got some painting pants, spattered with what they said was blood. They arrested him and beat a statement from him. He later told me he'd said, "No, I never stabbed this lady," but he was so tired of them—the detectives—stomping him, that finally he said yes, he did it. He was found guilty by a jury and sentenced to life, but years later, he was granted an appeal because he had not been advised of his Miranda rights. I will inject some of his writings into my story. He has given me permission to write about him. Denzel received his name from Mr. Lane as did my mother's the other children. I was named after Mrs. Lane and Linda after her daughter. Steve was named after another lady Mother worked for, Mrs. Bender. Denzel, my beloved brother writes:

I was a problem child, because if I saw something that I wanted, I would simply sneak around and steal it. I went from stealing cookies from the corner café to easing into downtown Atlanta to try out my new skills. My very first theft from a big store was some swim trunks from Rich's Department Store. Back then, instead of going to school, I would go to the front door of the school and out the back to meet with another delinquent named Peewee. We were birds of a feather because we both liked to shoot hooky and do whatever came to mind. One fine day playing hooky alone, I decided to go shop*lift*ing. I was around six or seven years of age at the time. I went to my favorite store, Rich's, to see what would interest me. I came across a purse sitting by a counter on the floor. Not knowing that I had been followed by a floorwalker ever since I had set foot in the store, I grabbed the purse and ran down the escalator, but it was the one going up. I found myself in the air by the seat of my pants. This deep voice asked me where was I going and whose pocketbook was I carrying. I turned to look at this person and all I remember was a big red face. I told the face that the pocketbook belonged to my mother. I was taken to some offices and photographed and asked was my mother a white woman. Needless to say, I was busted and taken to Juvenile Hall where I was put into a room with larger fellows who had committed crimes themselves. The person in charge told me to take off my clothes and take a shower. I refused, because I had heard from Peewee about what the bigger boys would do to you. So my clothes were forcibly taken off and I showered. My thoughts were on what I had seen happen behind the school in a wooded place called the jungle. There, it was said, some men hung out waiting for children to come through so they could grab them and rape them or make them suck them off. I was with a boy once and we went through the jungle. I heard a noise and hid in the bushes. He went to see who or what it was and had the experience of his life. One man grabbed him and put his hand over his mouth while the other one took his pants off. After a brief struggle and a few licks on the head, the boy did as he was told and sucked one fellow's dick. Then he was forced onto his stomach while the other man fucked him. All he could do was holler and cry. When they finished and left, the boy went one way and I hauled ass the other way. I never went through the jungle again.

The next morning, my mother came to get me and brought along a tree branch. She gave me a couple licks before I broke and ran from her, only to be beaten damn near to death when Dad came that night. I was taken to school the next day in one of my sisters' dress and made to stay that way the whole day.

My mom was a domestic maid, and I don't know what my dad did for a living. Mom used to take me to work with her. I got to know the people she worked for, because the man of the house took an interest in me and taught me a lot of things, mostly outdoors types of things, like naming small animals, *factory*s, and trees, and roasting chestnuts. He also bought me my first bicycle for Christmas. He told me if I made good grades and stayed in school, I could keep it. The bicycle didn't last long, because I had a rotten temper and was very destructive. I would tear up anything I could get my hands on when I was upset, which was quite a lot. I remember riding my bike down the street and the seat slipped off, causing my foot to slip off the peddle. At the time, I was standing up, and I hit the center bar on the bike. I swore that my nuts were busted. After rolling around in agony for a while, I got up off the ground, picked up the bike, brought it up over my head, and slammed it about three or four times. Then I walked away and left it. When I returned home, I was asked about my bike. I said it had been stolen, thinking I had told the perfect lie. I was cornered later by my older sister, who proceeded to blackmail me into going downtown to steal her a big doll and a sweater or she would tell Dad. She knew just what to say to get either one of us to do her dirty work. I took my youngest sister with me for lookout and picked out a pretty fuzzy yellow sweater and a big doll, and I got a small transistor radio for my enjoyment later on. This went on for a period of time, my oldest sister always watching us to catch us in the wrong so she could force us to go to town and shop*lift* for her. We usually hid the stolen items until we could lay them out in the open. Mom would say to my oldest sister, "Where did you get that doll from?" and she would say, "I found it in the alley." Things were easily explained away, but I think Mom knew what the deal was. She'd tell us, "Don't start hollering for me when the law picks your asses up." To me, that meant be slicker and faster than the store's floorwalker and the police.

I used to snatch the change from the cigar boxes on top of a stack of newspapers for sale at the *newsstand*. I don't know exactly how many times I'd been caught stealing by the time I was eight years old. I was a regular customer at Juvenile Hall. The courts got fed up with my behavior, took me away from the family, and placed me in a foster home. That was the most hurtful thing I had ever experienced in my young life. I had become numb to Juvenile Hall. It didn't faze me too much anymore —just another home to me.

I was placed in a home on Del Mar Lane with eleven other children, rogues who were in the same shape I was: sneaky, foul-mouthed, hurt, and confused. After the shock of losing touch with my family, I figured out how to adjust and make the most of the situation by doing what I was told, going to school, and going to church damn near every night. Life with Mrs. Hunter and the rest of the children was quite a learning experience. Her main program was plenty of church services and discipline. I guess she saw the devil in me, because every time she went to church I was made to accompany her. If I fell asleep, she pinched me until I woke up. I used give her the most hateful look I could conjure up, and she would say, "Didn't I tell you not to look at me that way?" I hated all adults who caused me pain of any kind.

When I was home with the family and the husband's drinking buddies wanted some cheap entertainment, they would send for me, since I had such a repertoire of sounds and could imitate most of the folks they liked to pick on. I was told, come here, boy, bark like a dog or talk like a duck, or show them how so and so walks. Afterwards they would give me a coin and tell me to be gone. I would go buy me some candy and try to enjoy it until I ran across some children who didn't have any and would try to take it from me, either by trade or by a girl offering sexual favors. Upon returning from church, I was usually told to go read the Bible and memorize a chapter before I would be allowed to eat the next day. Remembering Bible chapters wasn't too hard, because I loved to eat, and I give my foster mother due credit.

The other children had problems, so I would help them. School was a breeze for me, even though I had been out of school more than in. Learning wasn't hard once I set my mind to it. I've always been a reader. I was always reading car tags, counting everything I saw, and just being curious about things in general. After a few months, I kind of liked it at the foster home. The only thing though, I missed my family. There were a few times that Mom was brought out to see me for a few minutes, and seeing her only made the tears flow because I was very aware of how she was living and how I was living. I had my own bed, clean sheets, a clean bathroom, plenty of clean clothes, and I was eating very well and just doing better all around, while they were living in one room in a rat-infested building, eating welfare food, with very few clothes, no television, just catching pure hell, and barely existing. We were worlds apart, but if I'd had a choice in the matter, I would have gladly gone back to my family. But it wasn't to be, so I made the most of things. There was even a garden, and Mrs. Hunter showed the boys how to farm—plowing, *factory*ing, and harvesting corn, sweet potatoes, snap beans, peas, and okra. Me being me, I decided to sample a few veggies raw—potatoes and okra—and they were delicious. There was a huge back yard, plenty of trees, a stream, and a swing. I used to love to go out back, sit in the swing, and daydream about most anything. I turned into a loner. I stayed lonesome, and since I couldn't go home, I became acquainted with myself. I stopped stealing, cursing, and chasing the girls, because we were forbidden to touch our foster sisters. We got along fairly well. They occupied the attic and we had the basement, with the parents on the main floor. Mrs. Hunter shopped at places like the farmers' market, and with eleven children to feed, she knew how to do it. I used to like it when she would buy a big barrel of apples and set them on the back porch. I would just help myself until I was caught. Then Mr. or Mrs. Hunter would take me upstairs to get a whipping.

Since I fashioned myself a wanderer, I decided after one whipping to just leave and try to find my family. I guess I had a good sense of direction, because I found my way back. When I found the family, I broke down and cried. I had been living like a king and my sisters and little brother were in bad shape. But I was back home, back on the dirty streets for a few days. Mom told me that I would have to go back. When the social worker came for me, I was taken to Juvenile Hall until I could be placed again, and I ended right back with the Hunters, promising not to run away again. It wasn't long before I was back to my old tricks, raiding the garden and barrels of fruit. I recall one Thanksgiving that started out normal and ended abnormal. All of the children were seated, and everyone was hungry because we'd had a very light breakfast. We said our grace and proceeded to eat. Since I used to eat fast and wolf down my food, I asked for seconds of turkey, mashed potatoes, beans, cranberry sauce, and bread. I was told to fix it myself, so I piled it on and was finished before everyone. After everyone had consumed seconds, Mrs. Hunter asked if I wanted more, so I said, "*Y*es. ma'am." What did I have to say that for? Mrs. Hunter told me that she would fill me up that day and told me to eat the rest of the turkey. We really hadn't done any damage to it by slicing it up, so there was quite a lot of it left. I ate and ate it until it was gone and was so full I thought I would burst. I had a terrible night's sleep and was very uncomfortable the next day, but I pulled through and was back to my old self the next evening. Sometimes it seemed like the lady of the house didn't like me too well, so I would get anti-social and withdraw into myself. That became my trademark, and I became quite comfortable with myself and my thoughts. The only drawback to that was that I ended up with a permanent mark, the expression I used to wear, and I was asked quite a lot what was wrong. Most of the time there wasn't a damn thing wrong with me. I just wanted to be left alone. I didn't want to play or do any fun things. I would go out back and entertain myself in the swing. I guess the lady of the house started to be moved by my behavior and my silence, because I was placed in an orphanage quite suddenly. I was in a dorm with about fifty other delinquents, and though I always tried to fit right in, I didn't go out of my way to make friends. If it happened, fine; if not, better for me. Life in the home was quite different from Mrs. Hunter's place. Everyone wore the same outfit and there were girls on the other side of the building. We mingled and played head games with each other, but I guess we all had things we needed to straighten out in our heads. I was transferred to a new school and had a few girl problems. I really didn't want to deal with the girls in the home, so I started associating with the girls in school, and the boys didn't like that very well. But I was always being eyeballed and complimented by a few girls, so I followed up on a lot of the play I was getting, which led to my being confronted by one girl's brother and a boy who liked another one of the girls. I was threatened with an ass kicking if I didn't back off, so I went to war. To my utter surprise, the other fellows from the home joined in, and it was known from then on *that* no one messed with the fellows from the home. The people running the home were in the process of moving it to a new neighborhood when I came. About six months later, we moved from the ghetto side of town to the middle class neighborhood and from dingy dorms to four-person rooms. It was truly a nice change. There were lots of woods, and I discovered a new side of me. I used to love to walk in the woods, try to catch salamanders and crayfish in the stream, pick berries, and just enjoy nature. Then I found out I wasn't the only outdoorsman in the complex. The home consisted of four buildings, and we were placed by age: the younger children had a separate building from the older children, and the girls were separated the same way. But here in Collier Heights there was a lot of midnight creeping going down. I struck up a few light romances, not really being serious about them. Life in the new place was pretty routine. After the newness wore off, we all had our meals in the big dining area. There were dances on birthdays and holidays. School attendance was mandatory, and so was discipline. This was where we didn't see eye to eye—on being whipped with a piece of tire rubber dipped in water. I was whipped once and decided to cool out with the foolishness, like raiding other people's lockers, or cursing and fighting. All in all, we got along well with each other. It was the staff we didn't care too much for. I remember one staff member who was going to college to be a minister. We didn't respect him because we found out he liked boys. He used to wake up certain boys by rubbing them on the butt. Some liked it, and they used to play sleep when he was on duty. We were persuaded to play sports, which I didn't mind, because I had a fastball that was hard to see or hit. I had a bad habit of throwing rocks at anything that moved. I hardly ever lost a rock battle or a contest to see who could throw the farthest. One fine day, we were playing football in the complex, and much to my surprise, I looked up and saw my youngest sister. It damn near broke my heart. I hadn't forgotten my family; I just hadn't seen them in a while. We talked, and she brought me up to date on the other family members. All of us were in foster care, taken way from our parents, because we were ungovernable. I heard things like Mom was unfit and Dad was a drunkard. It's funny, because I didn't see them that way. The way we were raised in that place, it seemed normal to me because the whole neighborhood was the same. Well, time slowly passed, and I concentrated on getting out of elementary school, which I did, and went to high school—Harper High. I'd always had no self-esteem and was shy and withdrawn, but when I went to high school, it really came out. The other children at school used to pick on us kids from the home because we dressed alike and weren't with our families. We fought a lot, and didn't do well in school. I was placed in special education, reaffirming my old belief that I wouldn't amount to anything in life. I didn't even try any more. I would just go to school and wouldn't say a damn word unless I was asked, which wasn't often, because the other nitwits were very disruptive and they diverted attention from me. Eventually I was reassigned to regular classes, after I got tired of being constantly a shamed and watched like a dummy every time class was let out or we were in the lunchroom. Mom was somehow able to move into some projects in the West End, and I was released back to her. I had been gone for five years. I was fourteen-and-a-half and big for my age. The neighborhood where we stayed was integrated, and the Caucasian males dominated it—or did until an influx of black families moved in. Things were cool in the daytime, but if you were caught at night outside alone, you were fair game for the white gangs who roamed the projects. They caught me once, but I didn't suffer any harm because I was quick on my feet. When I was younger,

I used to run from the police and the truant officers, so I had some experience in the art of fleeing when scared. I did a few break-ins and found myself a small pistol, so I was no longer afraid to walk the streets at night in the projects. I became the predator and started stalking the white gang members. Once, during my nightly outings, I ran across a white fellow about my age who was alone. We watched each other for a while until he started a conversation, like "hey man, what's your name" and "do you live over here." I gave him my name and stated my street address and I asked him what was he up to at that time of night, dressed in dark clothes. With a sly, sneaky smile, he said, "Oh, I'm just out seeing what I can steal. After that night, we were inseparable for about a year. We became partners in petty crimes. He was a bold young man. There were times I wouldn't be home and upon *returning,* I would find him on the porch or inside talking to my mom or sisters. He was a regular guest. He would spend the night at our house, but I never spent the night at his place. His mother wasn't quite that liberal, but his sister was. She was fond of me and frequently invited me over when her mother was out or had gone to bed. We had some lovely times. We enjoyed a year of fun, spending sums of ill-gotten money, but then his family moved, so I settled down and started going to school more often. Soon that became routine, so I went back to the streets full time. I would go to homeroom, wait until first period, and then leave to go wherever my mind directed me. More times than not, it was back downtown, where I was getting involved with a crew of car thieves and burglars. We would steal a car from a lot, find a place to break into, take what we could, and spend the next few days trying to unload the goods. Sometimes we would get a decent price, but mostly it was a quick sell because any money was considered a profit. Things didn't work out between us because as the money started coming in, some of the fellows started getting greedy and demanding more, saying they had done more or taken greater risks. So I quietly slacked up on going out with them and went solo. It was better for me. because I've always had a sense of fair play, right or wrong. In my early teens, I used to walk a lot, casing out places to hit, checking out cars, and sometimes just wandering about. More times than not, I was approached by men cruising around looking for young boys to spend some time with, and yeah, as you can guess, since money was mentioned, I went along to see where it would lead me. It led straight to their homes, looking at dirty movies, getting drunk, and making the money, mostly by letting them give me head. There were times when I was asked to fuck them, and that only happened if the price went up. Since I try to do my best in whatever I do, I soon placed myself in various locations and was in demand where ever I went. The money was good at times, but there were times when I was tricked and didn't get what I was promised. But those shysters lost more than they ever imagined in other ways. I never beat anyone up over tricking or lying to me, but I robbed them out of house and home, and a lot of cars were messed up real nice. Trouble started when people started getting their feelings involved, when for me, it was purely a survival situation, so I slowed it down and started looking for some type of work.

I was fifteen years old, stood six feet tall, and weighed 225, so when I went to certain jobs, age wasn't a factor. I was usually hired on the spot for certain jobs, like construction and warehouse and delivery. I went to work every day. I was in the streets some nights, but all that came to an end when I was about fifteen-and-a-half. A murder was committed in the projects, and since I so well known and raised a lot of hell, and because I looked mean and had a rotten temper, I was picked up and questioned about it. I didn't do it. I had been with some other people, drinking and sniffing glue in someone's yard, a long way from the from the crime scene. The detectives came to my house and told Mom that they wanted to talk to me about the crime. She asked, "Why him?" and they said my name had come up a lot around the projects. At the time, I hadn't heard about it. I thought they wanted me for car theft. The police took me downtown and questioned me for a few hours, then released me. At some point or another I read about the crime in the paper, and I recalled that on that very same night, two acquaintances of ours had come up the hill and they had knives with some blood on them. We asked what was up, and they told us that there had been a fight down the street but that everything was cool. Thinking no more of it, I went on with my business of making money any way I could. I had been fired along with the driver of the truck for stealing furniture and selling it. Times were always hard; there never seemed to ever be enough food in the house. I think I had been street poisoned at an early age, so whenever I needed some funds, I knew where to find them—in the streets. About two weeks after questioning me, the detectives came back and put me in their car in front of the house. It was summertime—mid-July, and neighbors were sitting on their porches, shaking their heads. I heard a few muttering, "Tsk, tsk, there he goes again." We sat in the car about thirty minutes in dead silence. Finally, one of the detectives said, "You make sure you take a good look at this place and your mother, because your black ass is going to the electric chair for killing that white woman and stabbing those two white boys three weeks ago!" My mind went completely blank for a while. I knew that I didn't do it, so I started to do some real thinking. I came up with this brilliant idea that I would tell them what I'd read in the papers and would be set free at the trial. I was told about the electric chair over and over, until we went some place down town for a lie detector test. After it was over, I was told that I failed it, and they took me to police headquarters on Decatur Street. I was handcuffed from behind, placed in a chair, asked about the crime. I was hit repeatedly with a phone book from behind my head, punched, and stomped in the chest. They said I had resisted, which is kind of hard with your hands tied from behind. I told them exactly what I had read in the papers. They said that's what happened. I was charged with first-degree murder, and Mom was called down and told of my confession but was not allowed to see me because I was beaten to a pulp. When I did see Mom, it was one of the most devastating days of my life, seeing her tear-stained face. I tried to comfort her by telling her that it would be all right at the trial. She screamed, I guess because she knew better than I that it would not be all right. That only hurt me more, seeing her that way. I was taken to jail and placed in isolation, due to my age. I was in shock most of the time I was in jail. Being in a small cell by myself gave me ample time to think about the situation I was in. Lights stayed on twenty-four/seven. I re-read the Bible quite a few times. I was so full of pure hate for the detectives who had given me a murder and aggravated assault case, if the chance had of presented itself, I would have been guilty of murder if I could have just gotten my hands on either one of them. I knew the pressure was on to crack the case, since it was black-on-white crime. When blacks started to outnumber whites in Harris Homes, I could feel trouble coming, in the way of a lot of crimes were being given to blacks, whether they did it or not. This was 1968. I couldn't focus to properly in jail because I was too consumed with hate and impatience. The sooner the trial was scheduled, the sooner I could go home, or so I thought. Nothing eventful happened in isolation, mainly routine stuff: get up, eat breakfast, read for a while, eat lunch, wait for the commissary to be delivered, take a shower, eat dinner, and go back to bed. This was my routine until I was placed in a cell with other murderers. It was a relief to see and talk with someone and listen to all their bullshit. I didn't encounter any problems because I kept to myself and minded my own business. I carried myself like I didn't want no shit and didn't play no games and I was a product of the mean streets, meaning that if no one brought me no shit, I wouldn't bring them any. The usual questions were asked of me: what are you down for, and so forth. When murder was mentioned, some stepped back in surprise, and some said join the club! I learned all of the card games, craps, and I usually stayed glued to the TV. Some Saturdays, Mom would come to visit and leave me a few dollars on the books, tell me who said what, and always remind me to watch my temper and be careful. In about three or four months, I turned sixteen. I was given a date to appear in court. Mom had secured me an attorney through her employers, and I had two state attorneys. Copping a plea wasn't in the picture. I had plenty of witnesses on my side, and I knew that once the boys who were stabbed saw me, they would tell the truth. On the day of the trial, I had a chance to see the boys, and to my utter surprise I knew I both of them. They were brothers who used to come on the *ball field* and a group of fellows *and I* would play ball. They were never picked to play because they were to young and small. I told my attorney that I knew them, and they themselves said we had it in the bag. Boy were they wrong! The only thing they had on me was a confession that I gave them to get them off my ass. It was right from the article that was written in the newspaper. As the trial progressed and witnesses were called, I grew hopeful because I figured once the boys testified, it would be all over. They were asked and asked, did I kill their mother and stab both of them. I quote: "No, he didn't do it." Gasps were heard in the courtroom and order was called. The judge looked at the district attorney; he looked baffled. Mom had a smile on her face and things looked real good . . . until the jury came back with a guilty verdict! All of a sudden, I heard bells in my head and had to sit down. I couldn't believe it! All I heard after that was something about an appeal, and the judge said, "All I can do is give you is life in prison." My whole world came crashing down. I was stripped of my dreams, brokenhearted, and left with no faith whatsoever. Nothing was fair any more. No one could answer my question, why me? I knew I hadn't killed anyone or stabbed anyone. I was led to the holding cell to wait to go back upstairs. Then, what had just happened finally dawned on me, and I blacked out.

I woke up in the infirmary with a big fan blowing on my face. The doctor asked me if I'd gone to court and what had happened. I told him, and he said no wonder you fell out! I went back to my cell and everyone there asked how much time I received. I told them and went to sleep amid whispers of "damn they loaded young blood up, didn't they?" I was taken for breakfast, which I sold, and I picked over lunch. I was in a state of depression, and my cellmates respected it for about a week; then came the ribbing and advice as to how to handle an elbow (life sentence). It was said that every time you thought you had it straightened out, it would fold back up–every time you went up for parole, with hopes of getting out, you were denied, and that's after seven years! So for the next year, I settled into jail life while I waited for the appeal to be heard by a higher court. I looked forward to weekends because visiting days were the only bright light in what was a dark, dark existence. I also looked forward to new people coming into the cell; the old faces and stories had become all too familiar. Eventually, I was moved to another cell, due to a fight over my ass. Had it not been for this one old man, I would probably be a girl to them. They moved to another area that had boys my age and placed me in a position as sort of a monitor, or governor. A lot of bullying was going on and they figured that I could make a difference—which I did. I was given the job of houseman, one who made sure everything ran smoothly. I'd make sure no meals were taken or stolen and the cell was cleaned and would look out for the frail boys, take up store orders, etc. My reward for that was extra meals, extended visits, and phone time. This went on until one day in the springtime of the following year I was awakened by a loud noise in the cell and got up to see what was happening. One fellow in the cell told me I was getting out, and I told him to quit bullshitting me because I wasn't in the mood for playing, especially about that. He just gave me the newspaper.

Back to me . . . .

I will write more of the events of my brother. My life was more complicated now than ever. All I knew was that I had to control everything and everybody in my life. After the youth development center, I was mean and vicious and hated everything and everybody that crossed my path. This was a time of vengeance for me. I would meet innocent people on the street, and if they looked at me wrong, I would fight them. My mother and father were hopeless drunks, and they had teamed up with others who drank everyday shit that was made in the woods. Once I saw my father drink straight alcohol, the kind that you rub on your skin. My uncle Bo had come back around. This was Mother's brother, and he drank the same as they did. I hated every one of them. I would go to this house on Baldwin and ask Mrs. Pearl, "Please don't sell mother this shit." She ignored me, and I told her that she would be sorry if she didn't heed my warnings. One night, I went in the house and I had to use the bathroom, which was upstairs. There was a room at the top of the stairs, one of the bedrooms. The door was cracked, and I saw something. It was dark, so I had to turn on the lights. That sorry m-----f---er, her own brother, was rubbing Mother's ass. I could not believe what I was seeing. They both were pissy drunk. I went ballistic!

I turned around, and there in the hall was a small closet with a small pipe inside. I tore the curtain off of it, burst into the room, and began beating him unmercifully. He screamed and my mother woke up and asked what the hell was the matter with me. I couldn't talk. He was almost unconscious. I grabbed his head and rammed it into the concrete floor, satisfied that he was dead. I walked out the house and down to Pearl's. I looked at the drunks on the porch. I left, went to the gas station, and got me some gas. Then I went back to her house and set that bitch ablaze. I walked back to where I lived and sat on the porch. An ambulance pulled up, sirens and all, and about seven police cars. I was on the back porch. Mother saw me through the window and told them, "Here's this crazy m-----f---er." I didn't try to run. It wouldn't have done any good; there were guns everywhere. They said for me to lie on the ground and put my hands behind me, and I did. That had hurt me so bad, to see him touching her that way. It still does. They put me in the car and charged me with aggravated assault in the first degree. I was mad as hell it wasn't murder. So back to jail; too old for juvenile now. I am not sure what happened, but after awhile—a few weeks—I was released and charges were dropped. I never saw my uncle again. It was for the best; she would have been minus a sorry-ass brother.

Life only got worse—more fights. By now my sister had been introduced to heroin, and I saw a beautiful person someone I adored slowly turn to an addict. Hustling had become the norm for me. I was stealing checks from the boxes—any kind I could get my hands on. I no longer cared about anything.

I had fallen in love with Tony, and he was gone to prison. After my sweet days at Mrs. Russell's, I married him, but we slipped away and did that. His mother would never have permitted it. Once when we were in high school, Brown High, there was this girl named Cat who had a crush on Tony because he was a very good basketball player. She confronted me one day and I almost killed her. I had heard about her and him, but I just couldn't let her have him. Then I found out that he wasn't the nice guy I thought he was. He was just like any other horny bastard. Once, while he was in prison, I went to the home of a friend of ours for some reason, and being a mailbox bandit, I always looked at mailboxes. I noticed his handwriting on a letter, and I got the letter out and read it. Sorry bastard, this was his best friend's girl, and they had been f-----g for awhile. I asked her why. She got smart, and I tore into her musty ass.

My mother was getting sick . . . and I mean very sick. She couldn't get off the sofa, and Linda was getting strung out. I was out there and I was gone mentally, doing everything imaginable and some things unimaginable. Once, after the doctors said that she was going to die because her liver was gone, I stood there praying to God behind the curtains to just take her. I was pregnant, and he answered my prayer. One day, I was combing her hair. It was so pretty. She would never have allowed me to get this close. She always said that I was a dike, and she didn't like women. She would spit that snuff on me. But this time, being so weak, she gave in. The night before, this strange sound had come from her all night, but as I combed her pretty straight hair, she wasn't cussing, just sitting in that old orange chair. I said, "Well, I am going to let you sit on the porch." It was July 10, 1974 before 8:30 a.m. I waited to hear her cussing, but not a word came from her. She was gone; finally this soul was gone to rest. I thought back to the times she would scratch her legs until they bled puddles on the floor; they would not heal. I thought of the child that I was carrying, and how she never would see it. I remember when I told her that I was pregnant. She said, "I didn't know that a man could get pregnant." I wanted her to see something good that I'd done. I wanted her to see my child and then maybe she would love me. She loved my niece so much. So did I. Still do. She was such a warm spot. No one in our family ever showed affection until she was born. Once, when she was older, we found out that her and Sand had been stealing. I about beat her to death. I did not want her to live my life. She said that I put her in a closet. Strange . . . Harris Homes didn't have doors on the closets.

Back to mother . . .

Finally, she let me hold her in my arms, and I did. After a while, it dawned on me that she really was gone. I called my sister at work and my aunt. Denzel came into the house, and he saw her. Mother loved them so much; I wished she could have loved me. I later found out that her mother didn't like females or dark people, and I was both. They came and got the body, and my life spun totally out of control. I was already stealing everything I could get my hands on. We were stealing checks and breaking into stores. Now, once I went to the West End to a store that was in an isolated area. I went in, cased the place, then went to the saleslady, drew a pistol to her head, and quietly told her, "This is a robbery." We got everyone down and we cleaned the place out. At night, I would go places and throw something, break store windows, grab the jewelry, and run. Then I would rob mail trucks. Just out of control. This fellow that Linda had met was a villain and had introduced her to the drug, so her addiction was progressing, and I kept on robbing.

Once I went to this big dealer's crib. I had met up with this crew, and like everyone else that entered my life, they saw an opportunity to use me, my heart was unusually brave and strong to have been a girl so there it began. I was in the dude's house, and I had to get it under control. I had a sawed off shotgun, and I pulled it out and shot up at the ceiling. That got their attention. I had to let my partners in. I did, and we cleaned house.

One time, I knew this dude, and I had to set him up. He handled large—very large—amounts of drugs. He was also a numbers man, and he handled fake money. I went to him as if I was going to buy some money. As I was waiting, a knock came on the door and a name was said, and as the doorman peeped through the keyhole . . . boom . . . a blast! It was the crew making their entrance. They made everyone lie face down on the floor. I didn't trust these niggers with this kind of money, so instead of remaining like I was supposed to, I left with the robbers, kidnap style. Oh, no, not with that type of money. It could cause someone to lose his sense of loyalty. I also knew this dude was dangerous. I had to end up with more than a story, so I shot myself in the leg, trying to escape the robbers. I had statements to prove it. In all, it was nearly fifty thousand.

I began to tire of jumping over counters and robbing, so I got into counterfeiting. I'd met these fellows called the Miami boys. They terrorized Harris Homes and brought all manner of drugs in. I met this dude named Red, out of New York, and he had some fifty and hundred dollar counterfeit bills that he sold to us. Boy, that was a whole new bag! We were passing dollars untold, stealing checks . . . whew! Somehow, Linda passed a bad fifty and told them she got it from me. That's when the shit hit the fan! I was taken in and questioned, booked, and about to be sentenced because I was guilty as sin of everything. Being the brazen m-----f---er that I was, I didn't care. Let come what may. They sent my gangster ass straight to Alderson, West Virginia, to the big girls' camp house set in the hills, and things started to cause me concern. We arrived by air. The feds will fly your ass so that you arrive at your destination quickly. I was placed in Unit Seven, and the living arrangements weren't bad. Women from all over, no more county jail, no more small time hustlers. No, these were gangster women, masters at their games. The ones from New York, the District of Columbia, and Philly thought they were boss and ran the place. I heard stories untold, but they had some time under their belts.

Things for me were pretty smooth, because I really didn't take any shit. There was this girl out of DC and she was a boss, meaning she called major shots. And she saw something she liked and wanted. You guessed it—ME. Only problem was, I didn't like pushy hoes, and she was that—very dominant—and she usually got who she wanted. One day when I was down in the laundry room, I heard some girls. I thought nothing of it. Yes, in the past she would send me word of how she wanted to do me in bed, but I was too busy thinking of how I could get out and get back with Velvet Charon, as the women called him.

Before I got busted, I had met this fellow. At first he was so nice. His father was a police officer, but he was way too lame for me, and too slow. By now, I moved like a human rocket and left a blazing trail, so really, he wasn't my type. But on this one occasion, after we hit this score, a warehouse in downtown Peachtree, we went in and had to really hurry before the cops arrived. The alarm had gone off. Boy, was it a score! All kinds of fake furs and all kinds of kimonos, all pricey items. We offloaded the items and later went back to my place. A knock came on the door. I went to answer it, and to my eyes, this had to be the most handsome man that had ever lived! He smiled because I am sure he was used to women responding like that. I damn near jerked him through the door. He was looking for Alfred—that was my lame friend's name. I told him that he wasn't there, and he asked if he could wait. I said yes, and that's where it began. I couldn't take my eyes off him, and he was fine to boot. I found out he played football, and I could tell. So later, Alfred came by, and Vince asked what we were up to, making money? I really liked that he had some heart it. I was on, and he allowed me to fulfill any fantasy I had, rob any place with him right by my side. I asked him once to let me see him bang another man. He didn't exchange any words. I knew this fellow that got down that way, and he agreed to let him hit it. Now that I think back, I think they both enjoyed themselves; he stayed on the guy until he came.

Now, in the laundry room, it was quiet. Up came Linda, and she was not to be denied. Well, I had to let her have her way. I would have been punked until sentence expiration. Oh, no, that wasn't to be. I remembered back to my youth, and it was on. We fought and fought. She could hold her own, but my claim to fame was that I was a fighter. She pulled out two weapons: one was two more girls, and the other was a sharp as razor, which she used well. Every way I turned she hit me with it, and her cronies weren't missing many punches. I did what was best: I grabbed one of the girls around the throat with a chokehold and promised to kill the bitch if they didn't let me out. I was bleeding badly, but once it was cleaned, it wasn't too bad. They came and carried me to Davis Hall. This is where the rubber hit the road. I came out to shower and they kicked my ass like I was their child . . . but there again, I tried. We got extended time there, and they promised they would kill me. As we lay in there one day, the guards told us to get on the back wall of the cell. The only time they did this was when they were hurting someone or when someone died. So naturally, when they say don't, we did.

We watched girls being brought in, and later we found out through the grapevine this was the Charles Manson gang, who had committed the Sharon Tate murder. They were better off in Davis Hall. They would have been killed in the compound. They chanted, and we ragged the sorry bitches, being brainwashed like that. Never heard a word from them, unless we said something about Charles, that dirty lowdown ass. Then they would talk up and praise him; why, I will never know. Like he was some type of god.

I was transferred because the authorities didn't take life threats lightly. I was loaded onto another bus. This time, they drove me to Lexington Kentucky to a co-ed prison. I lived in the Renaissance Unit now. This was it. I worked in the medical unit. There were separate dining rooms, a place to go to the movies, and a place to skate. This was the joint! There was always excitement and plenty of money to be made. They paid you monthly on the details. Hell, it was a small amount, just enough to make something happen. The pay came in when you helped someone slip into a men's unit so they could fuck. I mean, they got down anywhere and everywhere in the huge laundry carts. Sucking dicks in the movies was an ongoing thing. Anywhere you'd see a crowd around, someone was in the midst of getting down. My girl was Lana Brown. When the funds were low, she knew what to do—go sell some pussy and hurry back. I was assigned to the hospital ward upstairs, and I made some serious money off the inmates that were there for federal protection. They couldn't eat the way they wanted to, so I would steal food; or when someone went on a furlough, I would have them bring back certain stuff. There was this dude named L. Mastrianni. He had a bad case of ulcers on his feet due to diabetes, I think. Anyway, he paid tops for everything from pussy to sausage, which he wasn't suppose to have. He told me stories of how the mafia worked, about the different families, and how he would give his girls Cadillac Eldorados and beautiful minks—just because!

One day, he asked if I was interested in some real money. I said of course. He told me to come closer and make him feel good again. I said, "How am I suppose to do that?" and he said, "Let me just put a tit in my mouth and slip off your panties." I said, "Hold on, big boy. I don't get down like that, but I know one who does." I knew his bank was strong, so I hinted, "She's pricey now, but she can get the job done." "Money is no object," he said, so I made it happen. This was the first time I had asked Lana to get paid this way. She frowned a little, but did it anyway. I slipped her up there. She stayed all thirty minutes. This was one of my ways of not getting close. If I knew you would fuck someone else for any reason, that was all you became to me, a means to an end. I went to him the next day and he requested her again.

Some of the people requested Talwin, a synthetic morphine: t's and blues. I would get them from the patients after surgery. Once there was a lot of static, and everyone was told to report to security. I later came to find out it was because of them bringing Mr. Leroy nikki Barnes through the tunnel. That's where they transported certain people. Now, I heard this from Pauli, who operated the elevator. He was also quite a figure. He was a handsome older man, hair white as snow, and diamonds on his hand big enough to choke a mule. Old Pauli liked the way Lana serviced him. There were quite a few fellows out of Detroit; they were gangsters, but what blew my mind was how they became bitches. They were snitchers and needed protection. No more big gangsters—just scared-ass old men that cried after surgery, after the pain returned.

The Jews had a separate dining area from the rest. They were holy in their view, but they liked to get their dicks sucked too. They always tried to get me to f--k them, but there was no way I would. Now, some of the women wanted them so bad; they would dress as men and risk getting shipped, all for a stiff dick. Then we were told that after the lights were out they humped each other. I know for a fact the women did.

For my leisure time, I would go out back and play handball. You hit this ball against this tall board in the heat. I got pretty good at it.

Time passed, and finally it was time for me to get out. I said my good-byes and the tears flowed, along with promises of seeing each other again. It was all lies. They would not let a person know until the last minute they had a warrant for their arrest for the state. My God, what the f--k! Damn! Struck out again! They were right there, handcuffs opened, and I was so shocked I almost lost my breath. Hello, you have the right to remain silent . . . the whole shit. I was still in shock. The charges were auto theft, credit card theft, possession of stolen goods, breaking and entering, selling stolen goods to the GBI in a sting operation in the year of . . . I was hearing bells by now. This can't be . . . *O*h, no, I don't know what in hell you are talking about. Whose name is on that warrant? It sure as hell isn't mine. Oh, but yes. it is.

They cuffed me and put chains around my waist. They drove me back to Georgia, where I was placed in the tank awaiting the preliminary trial. They read off so many charges, I could not believe what I heard. Looking back, one day we robbed a warehouse and had to leave before the alarm stopped. We scored. We'd heard about these white men who were buying any and everything we could bring. Now, that opened the floodgates. Niggers were robbing, snatching bags, going into offices, stealing pocketbooks, renting cars with the stolen cards and selling the rented cars. Everything they could move, they sold. This is where all those charges came from. I was right in the mix, always selling fake furs and silk gowns—whatever. They had encouraged us steal everything and bring it to them, but before they looked in the cabinet to get the crisp one hundred dollar bills, they would have you stand with them in this certain spot. Stupid, greedy fools that we were! They were posing us in front of the damn camera, taking photos that they were now using as evidence. No point in lying, saying that it wasn't you. Busted in the first degree. Now after all those years I'd just done, I must face this. A public defender asked for a bond. The judge just looked at him as if to say, you must be as stupid as they were. Bond denied. So we must await trial. Shit. Now came the deals. Hell, yes, I will take one look at my picture, grinning like a Cheshire cat.

I got two years in Hardwick Women's Prison. I immediately learned the ropes and blended in. It wasn't too bad a stretch. Back then, you didn't have to do much time, so I was soon released and sent to a halfway house. There was this honey that I met, and we hit it off pretty well. We got together and we both were sent to the same place. We got the 411 that this lady who ran the house was small in stature but didn't take no shit and did not like homos. Well, you know that I didn't give a rat's ass about what anyone liked, and as far as I was concerned, I made the rules. I slipped to Stellas room, and she quietly opened the door and let me in. I looked at her in her birthday suit, and I was ready for fun. We embraced and kissed. She was breathing hard. I don't know if it was from the moment or because she afraid, but we backed up to the bed and I began to caress her breasts, and I kissed her harder this time. She touched my breast and placed it in her mouth. That was what I liked, nice foreplay. I was taught by the best. She moved too quickly to the spot. I did not like that, so I pushed her off me and put my clothes on and left. The next day, I wouldn't even look at her. She insisted on getting me to talk, so around lunch, I did. I told her what she didn't do and that I was through with her. We were still in orientation, and I eventually allowed her to right her wrong.

Then I met this chap, her name was S. Bishop. She was so very nice, and I truly believe that she was just about God. We became friends, and she taught me so much about love, because she showed it. Now, this was still a time when I wasn't ready to adhere to society's rules and regs, so I was unable to see all that she offered, such as getting a life and being a decent human being. I was able to be honest with her about who I was and what I was about. She already knew. She was able to take us places in the free world—to the park and places where we did volunteer work, such as the Georgia Retardation Center, helping with the kids. I really enjoyed that. We had to help put them in the pool, and we could get in with them. They were so sad, but they didn't know what was going on. Eventually, I was given a job with them.

At the same time, I was getting involved with this fellow I had met at a dance at the advancement center. So that we would have some sort of social life, the halfway house would sometimes allow us to go to functions at the men's center, because they thought maybe that would keep us away from each other. I asked Stella if she wanted to go. She said okay, so we prepared ourselves for the evening. We were standing around the wall, just looking and checking things out. I got this funny feeling, so I looked around, and this dude across the room was staring so hard it drew my attention. I thought he was looking at Linda. She was very feminine and quite beautiful. She had pretty slanted eyes and a pretty smile. But a song came on and so did he. As he strolled across the room, I watched his every move—the way he walked and his stare. He had his eyes pinned on me. I thought maybe he was someone I had robbed, so I stood up and watched closely. I was kind of slumped on the wall, and soon he was directly in my face. Normally I don't allow strangers this close. He smiled and said, "May I have this dance?" I told Stella it was all right, go ahead. He said, "No, it's you that I want to dance with." I shot him a glance. Me? I was thinking in my mind. Me? I had never been approached so kindly and asked for a dance. To hold a sawed-off maybe, or to help get a house under control so it could be robbed, but never a dance and a beautiful smile to go along with it. Linda was checking me out, but I never gave anyone control over me. I did as I pleased and some that I didn't. I accepted the invite and went to the dance floor. I like to dance, I really do. The song was fast, and all of a sudden it got slow, so I turned to leave the floor, but he moved quickly and gently touched my arm and asked me to dance again, so I went back. Play another slow jam. This time make it sweet for my baby and for me, the words said. As he held me near, I began to feel a strange warmth. It was cold outside, but I was hot! So was he, for a moment. He wasn't the bad guy I felt wanted. I was catching feeling, but from where? I was gay, or so I thought. When the song finished, I came back to my senses and got a grip, and quickly exited the dance floor. Stella said, "Damn, I thought you would never stop." Another song came on; so did he. I again accepted, and this time he talked and I told him that I was with my date. He smiled and slipped me his number and name. Linda and I had words all the way back to the center about that dance. Anyway, we slipped into my room this time, and as we kissed, I couldn't get him off my mind. So I went to shower and bed.

I was outside sweeping, and there he was, looking at me across the fence that separated us. I looked back at him, and he made a sign for me to call him. I said okay. Later that evening, once I got a moment away from Stella, I called him, and the next day and the next. She knew something was different, because when she wanted to do me, I would not. Not like me at all. I was working on Peachtree by now, and he would come by. I could not get over how I liked him. When he spoke, I would get lost looking into his mouth, and when he held me, I could smell his sweet scent long after he was gone. One day he told me to meet him downstairs in the basement of the building. Bingo! That was it! I said okay, and I couldn't get there quickly enough. As I approached him, I felt the sudden urge to run into his arms. I did, and as he held me close, his pants got bigger and I swear I was on fire. The clothes were a lot to tear off, and boy that was nice! He stood there staring, and I got a quick glance at his body. Yeah, that was nice. I lay on the mattress and he followed, kind painfully at first, as he nervously held himself so that he could enter me. Even though I was quite moist, he still had difficulty entering, but it got better. He was somewhat surprised at my performance level, but what he didn't know was I had been thrown into a certain lifestyle out of need. Now, I not only wanted him, but I felt a need for him. Long after he was spent, I was still revving my motors. But we knew that if we didn't stop, we would end back in prison for escape. So we called each other and visited every chance we could. Linda got wind of the budding romance and hated me for it. We often went to his mother's house on pass and made great love or lust. It was great, because of youth, the newness of the experience, and that hot feeling inside. To this day, I can't explain the inner thunder and endless bliss. As we lay there, he whispered lies of loving me forever.

We were finally released. Remember, this was my second sentence. By now, Tony jr was about seven years old. I'd left him years ago with his grandmother. I had a little time with him before I went to prison. He was such a bright child! He would tell me, "I eat." That was his way of saying that he was hungry. I had him shortly after Mother passed, and as I said, that was when my life spun out of what little control I had. I had no skills or way of providing for him. His father was in Alto, confined, so it was on me to provide for him. My father, my brother, and my sister Linda had moved out with Frank, so it was just me. They never brought him to visit, but as soon as I was released, I got him.

♦♦♦

The rain outside is pouring, and so are the memories. As a young person I had issues with trust, and always looked at a person as, what next? Now I didn't have a place, so I had to return to Abbott Street in Harris Homes. My father was sitting in his favorite chair, the one where Mother drew her last breath. Along with me was my new love, and yes, there was a mattress and we occupied it. I had the job at Georgia Retardation Center, and I finally got an apartment on Skipper Place. Terrance wasn't working, but seeking, or so he said. I was just happy to have somewhat of a normal life. Or I thought so. One night, Terrance came home and said that this fellow had a way for him to make money. Happy with what I had, never really concerned when on a few occasions he would ask what I was in for, and not thinking anything of it, I told him. I also included the fact I was happy for it to be behind me.

Well, my lover had other plans for me, now that he knew of my former lifestyle. He came in late one night, dumped a very large sum of money on the bed, and told me to help myself. I had a strange feeling inside, and I did not heed the warning. The next score, he needed someone to watch and to provide a place to keep the money. Could I go with him? That one turned into over forty armed robberies. We were a modern day Bonnie and Clyde, from Georgia to New York and everywhere in between, jumping counters, leaping through windows—we couldn't go into a place unless we robbed it. From dope men to Steak 'n Ale, no one was safe. Then we met up with my old crew and it was on and rolling. Well, all things must come to an end, and one day we had gotten so bold, we didn't even wear masks. We went into this Kentucky Fried Chicken and ordered food. Before we left, we robbed it. I would see the fear on the people's faces. When we put them in the freezer, I would make sure that there was an inside knob so that they could release themselves. We were very fast, in and out. Terrance and I no longer knew whom we could trust or how to get out. We went into a Starvin' Marvin, maybe for cigarettes for me. He didn't smoke them, but he smoked plenty of other shit. On that last score, a smart bus operator got our tag number. You would have thought that it was Al Capone that was coming out the place. I have seen guns, but not so many at one time or so close to my head.

"Bitch, if you breathe loud, it will be your last. Get on the fucking pavement." I quickly did what I was told. Now it was my turn to look down barrels. We both were placed on the ground and searched. A man was searching me, and I said, "Isn't a female suppose to search me?" He said, "As far as I care, you are a man now. Shut the f--k up."

I mean, they cleaned the books on us: some we jobs we didn't do, most we did. We went to court many times, and we had a lawyer who represented both of us. Once the judge asked Terrance if I knew what was going on. He said, "Yes, sir, she did." I had feelings about that, but it was true. When we were to be sentenced, Terrance told the judge he had met God. The judge said, "Good. You will meet plenty of others before this is over. He then gave me a chance to speak. He said it would be just to give both of us life, but since we were so young and no one was hurt, he would give us twenty years to serve. It didn't faze me. I had been to the state prison before, and I'd met all the thieves and all. They were there when I returned.

I read in the newspaper that Wayne Williams had snatched a child in the area my son was, so now I was tripping. They transferred me out to prison. Terrance was also transferred. He had his mother write me, and he did also. One day, my name was called for visitation. I was more than surprised. Who was coming to visit me? They said that it was my brother. I said, "huh?" I knew that my brother was serving time, so I went up to visitation. I saw Tony first, then I saw Terrance, so I knew not to blow. I went to the table and he said, "I came to get you." I said, "Say no more. Give me five minutes to reach the gate and I am coming over it." I walked briskly back to the gate. It very tall, but I took my sandals off and scaled it like a monkey, shaking and climbing. Finally I got to the top, and I was shaking so badly the barbwire stuck into my hands and I didn't feel a thing. I stood halfway up and free fell. Tony said, "Run, Momma! Run fast!" I dove in the back seat and said, "Drive!" We went a little way down, and the whole damn area was full of people looking for me. I had hidden in the trunk. they stopped the car, I was sweating bullets from fear They talked for a brief moment and off we went, straight to Kmart to change and get a wig, then off to Six Flags, as if it was all right. I didn't ask any questions as to how when he said that he had to take my son back. I said okay. I really was happy to be away from that prison. A lot of shit was going down with the inmates and officers, of which I wanted no part. What started as excitement turned to pure horror. Everywhere we went, we always had to look over our shoulders. Then we were back at it again, the same old thing, hotel hopping, running from state to state. He began fighting with me, and I fought back. Also, I wanted to see my son for a while. His grandmother would allow me to visit, until I was placed on the Ten Most Wanted list. Then she said that I could no longer see him until I got out of all the trouble that I was in. I asked her to please allow me to see him one last time. I would visit him and have on a different disguise, but it didn't matter; he knew me. I would take chances and take him to the movies or out to eat. This one last time, I was permitted to visit him across the street in the park. While he was talking, carloads of detective drove up and came across the field, but they did not have their guns out. One of them came over to me and asked if my name was Eloise Edmonds. I said "No, my name is Venus. Here is my ID." He said, "I see, but if you will just come with us, we will get your prints and we will bring you back." Yeah, right. I looked at Tony and I couldn't hold back the tears. He said, "Don't cry, Mommy." I cried harder, because I knew that it would be years, if ever, before I would see him again.

I thought of Terrance and how he would come to pick me up after my visit. My mind went back to the fun times, like when at night Terrance and I would go to Piedmont Park to swim, and we would kiss and make love. Life was so sweet then. The park would be closed and no one would be there except a few thrill seekers like Terrance and me.

Night, walking dogs, all kinds, lovers, fags, I love you so much, slip into the water, the coolness, the lightness of my weight, so beautiful his smile, water dripping. This must be heaven, rolling in the sweet grass, laughing, running, playing, kissing, let's go home. Memories of yesterday.

♦♦♦

They returned me to prison to face an additional charge. I am sure that Tony's grandmother turned me in; they told me so.

Coming from the dining hall, a girl said hello and that she had something to tell me, but I had to promise not to escape again. That made me smile. I turned to see who was talking and I looked into the most beautiful blue eyes I had ever seen. Her name was Liza. She became my best friend and my lover. She was a talker. She had everything that I needed, and she finally showed me what real love was. She inspired me to finish school, and never did I want for anything. I loved Liza, probably always will. Her sentence wasn't as long as mine. She would get out and a few months later someone would send word that Liza was in ID. I would go and see what she needed. She had an awful drug addiction, to pills. She got out one time and met this fellow named Kirk. He was her sugar daddy. She really cared for him, but he always wanted her high. I hated him for that, but as always, she made sure that I had more than enough. He gave her everything material. One time she got out and had an awful wreck, almost died, but a few months later, there she was. This went on for years. Once, she really hurt my feelings. She was high and had lain with a friend of ours. I caught her, and she stood up and said to me, "I own you, nigger." I couldn't help myself; I almost beat Liza to death. The women pulled me off her. The fights grew worse. She was high and we were living in a drug dorm. Damn! She was at the house meetings, nodding like hell. No problem. Kirk had bought the warden and her packages were not searched. That's how the drugs came in. To keep me quiet, she gave me diamond rings.

Finally something positive happened. They let this really nice lady come in to teach us drama. Her name was Ms. Barbara Lebow, and she taught us how to write and perform. We wrote the play Windows, which was beautiful. We won a state contest and were permitted to go outside the prison to perform. That was wonderful. We met Mr. Frank, Barbara's love. She told me I was an oak tree erupting roses. I still don't know how to interpret that.

Time passed, and I went to a halfway house. This was ten years later, and I was beginning to feel the weight of prison. I didn't want any more of it. I was getting tired. I did some volunteer work at the Salvation Army, and after some time they hired me. I enjoyed working there. I met so many people just like me, except they were mostly men. They were kind and respected me as much as I respected myself, and that was a lot now. I shopped at the thrift stores for small stuff. I wasn't permitted to bring items into the center.

I still loved Liza. She was still in prison this time and was waiting for her time to come to the house. I later found out that she had met another woman and had feelings for her. I came in from work one day and there she was, as pretty as a ray of sunshine, but I could begin to see the wear and tear of the drug life. It didn't matter; she was there and all those years of sneaking to make love and wanting each other were drawing to an end. In a minute we would be free, and I could show her just how much I loved and wanted her, and prove that love—real love—could last beyond prison walls, and that all those years were not just a means to an end. No more looking into each other's eyes and having to turn away because of the passion. Now I could be the one to finally provide for us, instead of her having to. I so looked forward to the opportunity! We finally got a pass on the same day. I had a friend whose sister had an apartment, and we explained what was to be and how long it was to last. We arrived at different times. I was in bed when she arrived, and she didn't waste any time meeting me. During my times in prison, I allowed quite a few ladies to make love to me, but since I didn't consider them to be mine, I was not going to make love to them. That's just the way it was, and if you were a hottie, then you could call shots. And believe me when I state I was a number ten. Now, if and when I was served and they made my toes curl, then I served them a toy.

I learned that trade by accident. I mean making sex toys.. Women love them. I really don't think that over half the women in prison are really gay, because when you introduce the toy, they stick and stay, and will cause bodily harm if another tries to intrude. Now, Liza was different. I tried to use one on her and she asked me what the f—k was my problem—if she wanted a dick, she knew how to get one. She told me never to ask that of her again. It was only a test, which she passed with flying colors. Liza passed all my tests of trust, loyalty, and love. As time passed, however, our fantasy world was put to the test, and we both failed. As we began to make love, my mission was to show what was inside of my heart, and as before, it was outstanding. I felt the heat that emanated from her. It was as if she was on fire, and as the sweat came, with it came the sweet smell of lovemaking. This time, there were no guards to listen out for, no stopping for rounds, no time limit. I kissed her so hard she almost lost her breath, and we couldn't get close enough. After about two-and-a-half hours, I was spent. So was she, but she had to have the last say. I was lying on my back and my eyes were closed. I felt her gentle touch on my breast, and then I felt the heat from her mouth. My eyes remained closed. She weaved her way to mount me and gently kissed my entire face and then moved slowly to my neck and continued on. Then she stopped. I opened my eyes to see what the problem was. She was standing above me and was giving me a lap dance. I caressed her smooth legs and raised myself up to feel her moistness. Slowly, she squatted down and lay on me, moved my legs further apart, smelled my body and teased my clit. Finally, she did what she did like a champ. I couldn't hold back; I came and came. After about another hour or so, we decided that we had better head for the shower and get back to the halfway house. Finally, I was satisfied.

Time moved on, and I was under the impression that Liza was searching for a job, but Truth revealed itself: she had got back in touch with Kirk and was back on drugs. One night, I received a call; it was Liza on the phone. I said, "Where are you this time of night? You should be here. You'll get an escape charge." But she said words that deafened me: "I am not coming back." I asked, "What in the hell are you talking about, Liza? That's five more years. She said, "I am high, Eloise." It sounded as if she was miles away. I did not want to hear that. I begged her, "Please don't do it this way." But she said, "Why come back? My urine is dirty. They are going to send me back anyway." I said "Please let me try to talk to Mr. Stocks and beg them not to put an escape charge on you." So she returned and was sent back to prison. I found out that each day she would meet Kirk and give him sex. That crushed me. I was working at the Salvation Army, where I was supervisor in the phone room. There were men of every caliber there—lawyers, doctors, homeless, ex-felons, etc.

After I had been there about two years (my co-worker was the cupid in this), there was a fellow who checked into the center, and they placed him in the phone room. He was a really nice fellow, and smart. He always worked very hard and was very polite and respectful. I can't say enough about how kind he was. Once, he tried to ask me personal questions in a way so as not to jeopardize his stay at the center, but I really wasn't interested in any of his personal gestures. But now my co-worker thought just maybe I should listen to what he had to say. I was a dispatcher. I would sometimes get behind, and he would bring me chips or something. I was hurting over what had happened to Liza, so I gave in. He came as a friend who understood what was going on, and I could tell him the truth. I had long ago stopped writing Terrance, and Liza was my life now. So he played his cards right. In the evening, he would walk me to Five Points, and he would offer to ride home with me. I barked, NO. He asked if he could meet my family. I said no, I was so ashamed because I was in the halfway house and that was prison. I never told people where I really came from. I was so ashamed. Being from New York, he was rather smooth and insistent. One Saturday, as I returned to the center, I saw my son playing basketball. Surprised, I asked him how he had gotten over here, and before he could answer, Norman stepped from the side of the building and said, "I got permission and brought him." I didn't know what to say or think. "No more hiding the truth, he said. He already knew. Someone at his center had told him. What a relief! I wanted to tell him the complete truth.

Eventually, it was time for me to get out, and I had nowhere to go. My father had passed. I was able to lease my own place. I moved to Clarkston. My son was getting older, and his father had been released from prison some time ago. He was a drug addict, and he would steal Tony's money and all the nice items that I gave my son, so I wanted to get him from around his father. This worked out perfectly for Norman. He agreed to keep Tony for me until I was free. I agreed to pay all the bills. I would go there on pass, and eventually I got with Norman as a lover. I was so grateful that he was helping me to care for Tony, I couldn't provide enough. Well, one day, Tony showed up with his tooth knocked out. I asked what had happened. He said that he was over at his grandmother's and ran into a clothesline, not paying attention to where he was going. So I got him a tooth.

Finally, I came home. Things were great. I would buy items from the army—they gave a discount to employees, and I bought a car. Then I found out I was pregnant. Norman had always told me that he would love for us to have a child, so I was happy when I found out. One night he wanted to use the car, and I found out it was to take a group to the skating rink. I said that I had something to do—take my niece Markisha out. She was spending the night. He hit me so hard I almost fell down. Oh, no! It was on. She was so frightened, she cried to go home. Now Tony was living with me, and I wasn't treating him well at all. I was hard on him and wouldn't let him have much freedom. He was a teenager, concerned with falling in love. I lost Tony's love and respect. Things only got worse. We were fighting more, and he began to detest the sight of me. He would go away for days and come back in need of a bath and food.

My sister by now was totally strung out. Her daughter was selling her drugs. She saw Norman in Techwood and said he was a crack head. My God, how could this be? He was so perfect! Now the wedge was coming.

Tony finally ran away because, as he stated to his grandmother, I didn't love him. My whole world was turning upside down. One day, I was on the bus trying to get to work because Norman had my car. I looked out the window and someone else was driving my car. I was big and pregnant by now. I got off the bus, ran over to my car, reached inside, and grabbed my keys. The driver hauled off and slapped my face very hard. I held on to my keys. He was about to drive off, and a another car pulled in front of him. The driver told him, "Man, the woman is pregnant." I screamed, "This is my car! I don't know who he is."

"Bitch," he barked, "this car belongs to a nigger in the hood. I rented it." By now the police were on the scene. I sat on the street and cried. I cried for the loss of my son and for the stupid m . . .f . . . I had married. After I proved that the car was mine, I hurried to work down the street. Things were getting worse all around. I asked for permission to leave for a while, and I went to the projects and hunted for Norman. I was so angry now I smelled blood. I was told that a fellow that fit his description was in the next set of apartments, which were empty. I went in, not knowing who or what might be waiting. I saw a girl with two men. One was behind and the other one had his dick in her mouth and they were going at it. I heard a noise in the corner, and there was the love of my life with an antenna in his mouth. He didn't care that he smelled worse than a dog. He was farting and puffing. I saw a bottle lying there, and I broke it. I would have cut his throat had he not raised his arm. I screamed and cried, "why?" He wasn't thinking about that. He said, "I will give you your keys for ten dollars." I stabbed him, and he gave me my door keys.

The next morning I heard something on my patio. I opened the blinds. It was him, curled up like a baby. He said, "Please, just give me something to eat." My heart went out to him, and I let him in. He would come and stay a few days, then off again. I didn't know what to do. Finally, when it was time for the baby, he returned and we tried again. I had gotten huge, and he hated me by now, so I began to go to the school track to jog to lose weight. I was making some progress when one night he came and spoke only of love. I needed to hear those words from him. He said that he was sorry and he missed me. Even though I didn't believe a word he said, I was lonely and hopeful. He held me in his arms and kissed me. It almost reminded me of yesterday when he'd said that we were forever and promised to be my forever love. He touched me with desire, but I said I couldn't make love; it hasn't been long enough since the birth. He promised to be safe and pulled out a condom. After we finished, he just coldly pushed himself away and got up. Later that morning as I got out of bed, I stepped on the condom. I picked it up and sperm dripped from a hole in its tip. I found out at my six-week checkup that I was pregnant again.

Life was going from bad to worse. He wouldn't help with the baby and wouldn't work, so I was working everyday and paying bills, trying to think. My sister was getting worse. Her husband who had loved her so much once, now just gave her money to get her out of his face. My niece was living the fast life. She loved to go to clubs and just be young and wild. One day, as we sat together talking, she told me that she was pregnant. I looked at my sister, sitting there wearing one silver and one gold bedroom slipper, and I begged my niece not to have this child. Who would care for it?

"You don't tell me what to do and don't tell me to kill my baby," was her response. I thought, what is difference between mental murder and physical? My sister was so involved with drugs that her home was a shooting galley, filled with students from Georgia Tech, prostitutes from Ponce de Leon Avenue, thieves, crooks, and snitchers alike.

The baby was born with severe defects, and my niece had feelings of shame because the child was handicapped. She was over at a friend's doing whatever she pleased, and my young nephew was watching the baby. I was on my way to work, and I stopped by to see how things were. There he was, trying to attend to the needs of the baby. I asked where my niece was, and he said that she'd spent the night at her friend's. I asked where this friend lived, and he told me. I went to the apartment and there she was, laid up with some dude. I fought her, and she drew a knife on me and said that she hated me. I said, "I asked you not to have this child, so come on, let's go and see about her." She came to hate me, and in time, she would pay me back. Nothing was right. It was time to have the second baby and I had to go alone to the hospital and I brought her home alone. By now, Norman had found a temporary position at a warehouse, and that's not all he found there.

At home, the tension between us was fierce. He couldn't stand the sight of me, nor I of him, so the fights escalated. He was awful to my children and would hit them. Just before our daughter was born, at his temp job, he met a girl named Toni. He moved out and went to live with her. I went to the job early one morning after he had come back to me, but something just wasn't right. As I lay on the ground and watched the baby kicking from inside, they came out together. He went to her car and they laughed and hugged. A tear fell from my eye, because I could remember when he smiled like that with me. After I got up, I went to her car and asked him to please never come near me again. She said, "Who is that?" and he answered, "My wife," and he told me, "Please don't fight; you are pregnant," as if I didn't know. I knew from watching them that our love was gone, if it had ever existed in the first place, but he caught me before I got back to my car and begged me to let him come back. Did I have stupid on my forehead? Must have. I let him come back.

I had a young girl to keep the kids for me. One day, I came home and she was crying. I asked what was wrong. She said that Norman had tried to rape her. I screamed, and we began to look for him. Months later, he phoned and said that wasn't what happened. He left because he knew I would hurt him, but he agreed to turn himself in. He returned, and I was plotting on how to get away from him with the two children. I found a lady from the women's shelter to help with the kids. I gave her a place to live in exchange for babysitting. She was fantastic and faithful.

I still worked for the Salvation Army, and I had to work a half-day on Saturday. I received a call for a pick up. It was the end of the year. The caller needed items picked up, yet the driver's route was full. She said that she didn't care who came, so I sent a friend who had a pick-up truck to get the donation. It was old furs and stuff. My friend kept it on her balcony for a couple of weeks. She called me one day and said I needed to move it, so I put the items in the back of my car. One day, on a Saturday, I got to wondering about what kind of price furs would bring and thought that maybe I could sell them. So I got the yellow pages and began my search. I got a man on the phone and asked questions. He asked if I could let him see what I had. I said okay, I would stop by after work, which I did. When I showed him the plastic bag full of items, he said, "These are older than you." I smiled. He told me they would need to be reconditioned, whatever that meant, but he could give me a deal on a coat and would knock off twenty- five dollars for the old furs. I said "Let me look around," and I started to check out the store. He said if I didn't see anything up front he'd take me to look in the back, in the vault. I tried on a few coats, but they were too tight. And where was I going to wear a fur? In the back, there were coats wall to wall, all kinds and colors: mink, lynx, fox, and chinchilla. I saw a leather jacket with fur around the hood that I liked. He said that he would charge me three hundred for it, and I said okay. It was January and tax time. I told him as soon as I got my refund I would come back and get the coat. I was so happy that he said he would give me a discount on the pretty coat! I hadn't bought myself anything, really, since I was released, because I'd started to get furniture for the apartment. I was so excited! Finally, I could begin to live again. I had my son and the possibility of hope, but sometimes things don't work the way we think they should. My reality was that I was in a low paying job, married to someone I really didn't know, neglecting my son by not giving him the time and love that he needed, watching my beautiful talented sister walk the streets in search of drugs, and watching her beautiful child hurt for her. I had no life. I was starting too many things and not completing anything.

♦♦♦

Terrance came home and never even asked what had happened or why I discontinued communication with him. He had thrived and had great success. Yes, I regretted the move that I had made here. I had nothing. I'd seen the loss of control, but for the sake of my small children, I held on. Norman was hopeless and strung out to the max. I allowed him to take my son with him to a Narcotics Anonymous meeting, and after so many hours, I began to worry. He called me about three in the morning talking about if I ever wanted to see my son again, I needed to get money to pay this nigger, because while he was at the meeting, he stole my baby. I couldn't believe this shit I was hearing, but I told him to give me time to get to the ATM and I would give him the money. Strange . . . he wanted the exact amount that I had in savings. I saw the game, so I played it. The only thing I went and picked up was a nine-millimeter and bullets. I had come to the conclusion that he needed to be dead, because he wasn't fit to live. I approached the spot I was told to go. I had been told to lay the money in a certain place, and my son would be there. Sure enough, the stupid bastards were in place. I had some money and a trick I learned back in the days when I wanted to get in a house to rob it: real money was on top, fake in the middle. The dude brought my son out, and I got him just as the dude was reaching for the money. I shot his hand he screamed like a bitch. That sorry-ass Norman ran, but I went to the man and put the gun to his head and was about to pull the trigger. My son began to scream and cry, so I walked away and we went home. I was so hurt and disappointed. That's just a glimpse of my agony.

Now, back to the coat . . .

As the days passed, I filed for a rapid refund, and one day, as I often did, I stopped by my sister's and there were junkies wall-to-wall. She was upstairs getting off (shooting drugs), and it was a waiting process. I sat and waited. The people who were in the kitchen smoking crack had been told long before by Linda that if I came by to just act as if nothing was happening until I left. One of the young white boys from Georgia Tech came out to entertain me while I waited. He said, "What do you think Bill Clinton will do for the blacks once he's in office?" I knew that he was being smart, so I said, "I don't think that he will do a damn thing more than the rest have."

"Why do you say that? he asked. I said "Shit is still going on that was happening in days past, like way back in the fur trading days. I was in this shop just a few days ago, and I was told that we could barter a deal on some old furs I had and get a discount on a new jacket. Now isn't that what happened in days of old? So really, nothing has changed." We continued to talk, and I went on to tell more about the store and about what I had seen.

A few days later, I received a call from one of my nieces who said that she needed money to pay her rent and they had a score in mind, a robbery. I told her that I wasn't into that anymore, and I hadn't done anything but work since my release. By now, my sister's husband was into drugs also, which was a shame. He had been the backbone of the family. When I refused to participate in the robbery, they asked him, and to my surprise, he agreed. Linda had to go to night court. That was the only reason she wasn't in on it. As I stood in the living room, my niece and her friends prepared to go. I knew they didn't know what the hell they were doing, and for real, I thought that they were not serious. But I found out that they had been hustling together. Not only that, I found out that my niece had been selling drugs to the whole family, even her own mother. Even though my mother had hated the ground that I walked on, I don't think that I could ever have sold her drugs. All money is not good money.

As they entered the fur store, it was a cold January night. One of the girls was to walk in front of the store, stand at the bus stop, and be the lookout, while my brother-in-law and the other girl were to go in and buy a fur, and not seeing anything in the front, go to the back to look. Two more would come in, posing as customers, and have a seat on the sofa in front. All was going according to plan as they entered the vault. Hidden from view in the back, someone placed a pillowcase over the storeowner's head and a held pistol to his head. They made him lie down and tied him up, but they agreed not to take any personal belongings, only the furs. It was going just as planned. No one entered the store, and it was gravy. Only the expensive ones were to be removed. The clock was ticking, and finally all the furs that could be carried were loaded into the trunks of the cars and any place that a coat would fit. Unknown to them at the time, there was an eye-witness whom no one had seen, who supplied the police with descriptions of the robbers.

Now, my brother-in-law had become a crack smoker. Let's talk about that a little. As I said early on, he was the backbone of my sister's household back when life had meaning and purpose and hope of a bright future. That dream was gone, given way to defeat. Now the very thing that he hated had become his new bride. A heart can only be so strong. So the score was made, and the getaway seemed clear. As they drove, they placed a call to me and told me the details. They asked if I could get rid of the goods. I told them to come over we would talk. They had about seventy-five beautiful furs of all kinds, sizes, and colors—over a hundred-thousand dollars worth, the report said.

I was a known person in parts of New York where merchandise like this could be fenced, from my days gone by, so I agreed to get a U-Haul and make the arrangements, not fully knowing that my brother-in-law was as strung out as he was. I was so surprised the night we were at my sister's and my niece begged to be a partner, as did her two friends. I should have known better than to deal with any of them, but I made an exception because it was family. As we talked, I heard their desperation as they asked me to hurry and at least sell a few now.

About a week later, I received a call from my niece's aunt on her father's side, telling me that the baby needed Pampers. It was a Sunday. I had sold three of the coats to some drug lords who had that type of money on hand, and I was to turn it over to them when we met. But that was not fast enough for them. They gave no thought to me having to get things straight with my job for the trip. I rushed out to Brenda and gave her about two hundred dollars. As I was about to leave, I backed out of the driveway and damn! So many police! It brought back painful memories and it flashed back to Terrance and me. But not to get lost in the past . . . I quickly got a grip on my senses this time. The detective put his foot on my neck and put pressure on it. I was searched and handcuffed and placed in the back seat of the car.

Now, who knew that I was coming? Only one person. I'd thought about the night before, when I sold the coats. I'd had to sell half /half—one part was cash, the other was drugs. I didn't know who I could trust to hold it for me, so I thought, well, my sister sure can't keep it, and not her husband or Norman either, so that left me. So I wrapped it in a Pamper and laid it on the front seat, and it was there when I got busted. The car was impounded to look for fur fiber. The detective said, "What do you have to say, mastermind. I was dumbfounded; you could have knocked me over with a feather. I learned a long time ago to listen to what was being said by the one doing the talking. He said, "You will never plan another robbery." I continued to listen and really thought that he was just trying to scare me, but when he called my niece's name, I looked up, and all kinds of feelings and thoughts crossed my mind. But I still couldn't say anything; that was my family he was talking about. He then said, "Well, you just continue to be quiet, but by the time you're released, your next robbery will come from the senior citizens' ward. I had a seven-month-old and an almost two-year-old back at home. I only accepted the deal in the first place because I desperately needed to leave Norman but didn't have enough money, with two small kids both in Pampers. When I got to the station, everyone was in separate rooms, and mouths were flapping. Stories were being told. The first to squeal gets the deal, so I was given the charge. The storeowner lied and said that when I came to his store I looked suspicious. I was booked for armed robbery. As I got more details on the bust, I came to find out that my brother-in-law had taken a Rolex from the man's arm and was with an informant, and as they smoked crack from the money that was taken from the man's wallet, he'd bragged about the score of countless furs. Once they finished . . . Sonny was his name . . . he made a straight run to the police to inform them of the news he had of a fur heist. The detective had come to rely on this snitch's word as truth, so he investigated the information. He went to the apartment door and flashed his badge. My niece answered the door, and he asked to speak to my brother-in- law. She then said, "I know what you want to speak to him about." The detective asked her, "What can you tell me about a fur store robbery?"

"Everything I know," she later said. The reason she did that was she sold crack and didn't want them to search the place. Everyone who was in the house was taken down for questioning, and they wanted to know who had the furs. In unison, they chimed, "Eloise." My name was fed into the computer and the thing hit bingo. The detectives wanted me. That made sense. My niece was the first to give them my name. That was payback for all the times I had interfered with her young life. One day, after many months of waiting for trial and endless pretrials, we were sitting in the tanks. This time, I was alone. I stood up and looked across the hall. I saw my brother-in-law talking to the DA. As he was being placed back in the tank, I knocked on the window. My attorney told us not to take a plea bargain, but I was afraid it was too late—I'd heard too many threats of a life sentence. He never looked my way after he talked to her. When I stood before the judge, I changed my plea from not guilty to guilty, the reason being I could never have won a jury trial due to my past record of armed robbery. So I was sentenced to twelve years, instead of the twenty that the DA recommended. The judge said that from hearing this case over the period of time, he knew what was taking place. Everyone did. I'd already lost one child because of my poor decisions and going to prison, and now was losing two more. Thunder was crashing in my head before trial. I had Norman to go and get my car. Thank God the authorities never found the drugs! I contacted my son because I had some money hidden that I trusted him to take care of for me. He was given the remainder of the drugs that Norman hadn't smoked up. I would never have given his child drugs to sell, I don't care what, but he did. My son took the drugs and sold them with his friends. Never gave me a hello.

♦♦♦

I went in weighing around two-hundred-thirty pounds. Later, when I was weighed at the prison, I weighed about one-hundred-forty pounds. I worried about everything, especially my children. Once I called . . . it was on the weekend . . . and I never got an answer. Donna was the person who helped me during the week. She'd had the weekend off, but when I called back on Monday, I found out the babies had spent the weekend alone, and my son was one that was fascinated with electric sockets. I thanked God that he wasn't electrocuted. Anyway, I begged her to please never leave them alone, and she could have my income tax check for keeping them. She was so kind, she must have been an angel, because she even went to New York with them. When it was final that I was not coming home anytime soon, I crossed that fine line between sanity and insanity. Everything was a blur. I couldn't eat or sleep, and I often heard my heart pound in my ears. I cried, not just for myself, but for my sister and my kids. At first I wasn't bitter. Yet, I was numb, and as each day passed, my heart and emotions grew colder. The other girls were sentenced to less time, and daily I had to see them, talk with them, and continue to be family. I never forgot that it was my decision to associate on that level, and I had to live with it. I had been to prison before, but this was the time that broke my spirit. I wanted no part of this world, but here I was, totally insensitive to many emotions, unlike the time before. I had gotten older and now the pain was severe, whereas before, it was let's make it happen. I was forever explaining why and how I came to know of the store. Over and over, I told my story. I would smoke like a train, back to back, and run endlessly around the compound. Nights were long and sleepless. I could not believe what had taken place. Over and over my life flashed back and forth, around and around. I went over the entire process, still not grasping what had happened, what twelve years, what about my babies? I knew Norman would not care for them. Before court, I constantly prayed for a break. But I can remember praying like that each time I was in a jam never keeping my end of the deal, playing games. Now you know that I must have been one mentally ill human being trying to manipulate God. I sat here in the same situation I had been in before, yet worse this time. I knew loneliness; I knew pain; I really didn't feel a need or reason to live. My children were gone. The man I loved never loved me. What was I to do? Which way should I turn? No possibility of freedom.

The women were extremely loud. It was like being in a asylum, women walking with coffee cups, smoking cigarettes, constantly looking at the TV. Hating that I was ever born, I often wished that I could crawl up into a dark hole and die. How could I do this time? No one cared . . . no one to tell of this endless pain. Sleep, distorted dreams, looking for mail that never came. He'd left me before the sentence was passed. Slowly losing my mind, I thought back to the children who lived in the retardation center and I would see the things that they did, like one boy would read the news paper backwards, and I could see those that had lost their minds, continually banging their heads against the wall, biting themselves until they bled. I often cried for them; now I cry for me. Where was God? Did he finally give up on me? I am locked so deep inside, buried in the pain of my own, personal, tormented hell. I heard laughter long ago; was I ever in my life happy? I think not. I remember you, Norman. I don't like to, but I do. Never would I ever in my sickest dream have thought that you would leave me defenseless. Only you knew of the true love that I have for my babies. Why, Norman, why? You deceived me like no one before. Sitting in this cold smoke scarred room, fifteen feet long, seven feet across knowing that once again my right to life has cruelly and unjustly been taken from me, viciously and unmercifully. And me without proper knowledge to regain it or sincerely fight in its behalf, listening to endless pleas of injustice from the women, looking at the purple stained bed, my bunkmate trying to sleep her troubles away, trays up, a loud voice, idle chatter, doors slamming . . . huge steel doors, looking out the window that's about as wide as my hand sideways. Is medication here yet, she wants to know, so she can sleep more. Sitting in church the guests, they are not so fresh, the smell of burning cigarettes, bad breath, funky unwashed butts. The worst by far about this life is the lost of personal privacy, sitting in the open defecating and doing the personal stuff, changing. People standing right over you trying to use the toilet, talking, eating whatever the guests bring in, the smell of free air! The speaker is talking about principle, practice, position; it's so hard to concentrate. The girls who put me in here sitting directly to my right. I am capable of reaching over there and strangling them. They know they crossed me to the max. Yeah I am capable of doing some bodily harm to each one of them, but there is something inside that will not allow me to release my fury. If I was to harm or kill them, would it bring back yesterday when I was with my babies and Tony loved the sight of me? Would they take back this sentence? Too many regrets. Eloise, please don't be mad, she said in a letter, I had to do it. They said that I would receive life . . . but it was so easy for you to give me life, Linda. You must know that even though you are not here, you're saving lives. Eloise don't shut that door, she was talking about the cell, but I am fighting not to shut the door to life. Poor Brionna, I wonder if you know how my heart longs for you. No, you're only seven months old. Tony and Norman

Jr., I can't bear to even think of you; it hurt beyond words. Smoking cigarettes one after the other, which way do I turn? Who can help? Thoughts of God, some relief, looking at the calendar, it was moments then days, now months, visions of yesterday, sorrows. I don't feel like I am so strong, and I have never entertained fear, but I am afraid. How's Linda? Is she well? How is Norman treating my babies, are they being mistreated? Does he help Mrs. Carol with the care of the children? I doubt it; there were times when I had to take them to the Laundromat with me, along with the clothes. So many unanswered questions: Why was I born? Am I living out a ancestral curse? Why did Momma die? I never said that I was sorry for the many troubles I brought her way. What will his decision be? A miscarriage of justice, who miscarried justice, me or them or both? January 21, 1993 around 6:08 p.m. "I hope that she hurries, I hate to be rude, she's filing tax returns so white so dainty, so exceptional, next! Excuse me. My name is Eloise Edmonds. I called earlier inquiring about my return. The lady at the office said that it should be around six or there shortly after, looks at her watch, no he hasn't come ye, but I'm expecting him any moment now. 6:13 p.m., no show, excuse me again ma'am, what's your name, I hate to keep calling you ma'am, Ms. Margaret Dolby, it's been since the fifth. It's the tenth and I'm under the impression this should only take five days."

"Well, things are moving a little slow, preparation complications probably," she tells me. Can't wait longer, car is in the street, check back tomorrow. Damn, they charged, but no show. Driving home, frustrated, need my money, shit, going on vacation, I need a break, eyes getting bad, don't like driving at night. Home at last, come here Boonan, stop getting around those sockets, if you don't I will give you a few licks on those pretty fat legs. I'm hungry, um, chicken Cajun style. The phone rang. Eloise, it's Lady y. Can you handle something for us? What's up? I'll tell you tomorrow. Okay, see ya, click the phone, you look good, so what's up? Look, we've got some pieces that need to be moved, do you know anyone with plenty of money? What ya got? Let me make a few calls. Look, I have some nice pieces that I don't know how to price. I trust you to tell me what's fair. Okay? We're hungry. I have some Cajun chicken that Donna cooked. Damn, these are nice! I can't get what I want for them in town so I need to run to New York, but we need some money now, damn don't eat my pot. As soon as I hear from him I will let you all know. Friday, going to work, count time, brought back to misery. It's all in black and white. Why don't they check my story out? I couldn't have been in two places at the same time . . . I am not magic. No, I have the record, so it's open and shut. Return to prison. I just don't have the stamina as before I can't play this game anymore, the survival games of prison where you hire out. If you don't have family support, pretending so much until you believe the lies, love that only is real in prison, selling your soul for commissary necessaries, get in where you fit in, two for one, yard calls, listening to ridiculous lies of yesterday. Hell prison life will let you be whoever you want to be. You could be kin to famous stars, you could have been the wealthiest person and had the finest of everything, just a little down on your luck, the reason you're broke. But if you can tell the most convincing lie, wine and dine a lonely rich girl, walk to meals with her, make sure you have that store list to her the day before so that you can illegally pass it the day of store privileges, and you can have the best of both worlds. If you find a staff person that don't have a life or just wants to fuck a prisoner because there is no heat at home or if you get a really hot Bunkie you can do them all. No, I don't have the strength to participate. Just trust in God and everything will be fine. Waiting on my guidelines. Prison is a breeding ground for sickness, if the staff likes you you're good to go, but you must believe that nothing is free . . . nothing. Even their liking you, of course it has it benefits, like you and your people can go and get laid as long as your family is sending the staff money or humping them after light s are out, or when you have been assigned to wax and buff before visitors come. Inspection, stand at your door at attention, you better not fucking breathe. If you don't want to make parole they scream. Hell you are not going to make it any way; I don't have the strength to play this game anymore, unlike before, no Liza, no Lana. I feel like a wrecked ship that has lost its way. I should have known that my life would come to a tragic end. How could I have been so stupid? How could I have known? Maybe I am retarded in a way that no one knows. What's wrong with me? Perhaps that fall when I was only a toddler, now its effects are showing. I did too many people wrong. How did I honor my parents? Honor thy father and mother. I broke every commandment. I broke all the rules. I defied God, yet I always ask for his help. You shall reap what you sow, now that's true. I am my own worst enemy, my mind is sick. Now what have you done? You're right back where you started from, Ms. Know-it-All. Why did you have those kids, so that they could suffer from your neglect? What kind of life did you and Norman plan for them? How can you even think of blaming your mother for how you were reared, you are doing the same damn thing. You have been so selfish! Look how you did Tony. You were very mean to him, he wanted to love you, but you made that impossible. What about the time you took him out of the basketball team, you knew he was an excellent player. You say it was to get him to do better in his school work, but why didn't you listen when he tried to say you were hurting him? How you acted toward him and the other children, how you were more interested in falling in love than in building a relationship with him, you sorry-ass bitch. You deserve everything you're getting and then some. Now you have brought two more innocent beings into the world to be mistreated. I hope that you lose what little mind you have. You're not the fucking victim here, bitch. You are dead-ass wrong. You are cruel and will suffer for the rest of your life. Yard call! It's hot, maybe eighty degrees. I must run I must get away from Eloise inside my head, she's driving me insane. I am back where I swore that I would never come back, in prison. Did I ever leave? Some of the same faces. Damn, she's still here, she must have done over forty years, just as crazy as ever. They don't have a clue as to what going on out there prison. Life is not like free life. We're protected and so unprepared for the world. Time goes on. Hell, when you get out, you are out of time. I am waiting on my guidelines. It's another day in prison. I jogged and I watched the movie "Mrs. Doubt fire." I learned that once you lose what you have and say that you'd love to regain it, it takes skill, and if you and your lover part and there are children involved, every move must be careful and planned. August 24th, when I was sentenced to these twelve years, the situation was so delicate, the results left behind a trail of hate, pain, frustration, fear, very salty bitter tears. What little family I had died for me. I'll write again tomorrow if God is willing and I survive the night. It was in January and I had not long got out of the halfway house. I had married Norman and found out that that I was about to have a child, and also found out that all that Norman had told me on those many walks was lies and he was nothing more than a weak-ass crack-head, that's why he was in the Salvation Army. Lady y, why did you call me? Was it so wrong for me to try to tell you were living wrong and I didn't want to see you go out like that? Lady y, you are young and when you're young you think you know everything, as I thought I knew everything, and now I've I come to find out I don't know anything. I know that you feel like Falinda loves Lady c more, but just look at Linda . . . .She was so beautiful! Look at her now. Her life promised to be the best, but damn it, look! You hate yourself because you say your hair won't grow, but it's pretty anyway why can't you see your beauty? When I came home from prison, how do you think I felt when I saw the shape that my sister was in, wandering the streets all night long, just for drugs. I was the street person, not her. How do you think I felt when I saw Pooh crying because he didn't know how to give Angel her meds while you were laid up with some worthless-ass nigger? What right did you have to end my life? Linda was my best and only friend. I did not like how you all treated her. Dog, may you rot in hell for introducing both me and Linda to heroin. Now I don't know if I will ever see her again. What did my babies ever do to you? I guess you said to hell with them also. And as for as those sorry-ass friends of yours, they have you to thank that I don't f-----g snatch their punk-ass heart out. You all got had away. I'll never understand any of this. May 23, 1994. I received two birthday cards from the kids. That really was nice. My friend Betty sent them. I remember sitting in the gym in Hardwick waiting to be transferred to Washington State Prison. The women are being moved because there is big heat on the prison. Finally the dirt has made its way to the surface, fucking these inmates for gum and cute panties, having kids by them. Cason v. Seckinger, they called it. What good will it do?

The same thing will happen. Do they, the official, really think this will stop, or are they just doing something to please the public? It seems to be worse now than back then. I remember once a guard told me he had watched me and wanted me. I told him to go to hell. One night, as I was going to the clinic, he made his move. Me being who I was, I was ashamed to tell. But when we were in the gym, I was sitting next to this white girl and she couldn't stop talking. I think she was scared as hell, that's why she wouldn't stop talking, so she turned to me and this time she was trying to find out which way I was going so she could do some choosing. I'd seen it all before so many times. The first thing the women will say is, I don't know how these women go with each other; that's to see where you are with it. I wasn't in the mood so I said I don't either, but she had watched me before. So she kept her eyes on me. Sure enough, we went to the same prison in the same dorm. Bingo! We became very close. She didn't know how the game went so she was satisfied with a game or two of Scrabble or Acey-Deucey and a walk to the dining hall. She loved her kids and spoke of them often, and her husband, Ken. I watched her as her family drove her off the grounds to take her home. I did miss her, and she promised to keep in touch, and I'll be damned—she did. That is a common practice in prison, snot flying, lies being told of keeping in touch, but she did. I thank her for the card; they are nice. Woke up at 5:00 a.m. so that I can go to sick call. I need to do this so that I can receive glasses. I am seeing double, and everything is getting fuzzy. Count took from 12:30 to 2:00 p.m. to clear. Played softball, team was fantastic; they won 22 to 10, kick ass, huh? Talked with my niece concerning the Bible and tattoos. Thought about the kids sometimes. As I think of the kids, I remember when I called home and got no answer. I called back the next day, only to find out Norman had abandoned the kids. How could I have been so fucking stupid? I really don't know why I was so in love with him. It sure wasn't the sex. Hell, I ran circles around that bastard in bed. I will give him this: he was an excellent liar. He was real good at that, ran the yard heat high. but not near as hot as I am. Death, life, and real life issues. As I talked to Tony on the phone yesterday, he appeared to be happy. I called; he was concerned. Why I was shutting everyone out. I could never explain that just hearing of his voice ripped my heart to pieces. My God, what have I done? Oh, what a mess I have made. My being here . . . well, my life was traded out. As we stood in court and my lawyer said that we are pleading not guilty, Anita Wallace the assistant DA, said that she didn't care how we pleaded; her case was made. She had enough statements to send my ass to neverland, and she did. They told lies and gave me the case. Once, long ago, I left Terrance alone after we had completed such a long time in prison, not fully knowing if he really loved me as he said that he did, or if it hurt him me leaving to go to another. But if he did, I now know how it feels, and it is unbearable. Had it not been for Terrance, I would not have a lawyer. Shit, Norman pulled out before the gavel fell. I am slipping into another state of depression; here comes that darkness and those voices again. God, please help me! No bitch, what about when you put pistols to people's heads and they were so afraid that they cried. Did they deserve your treatment? How many times must I tell you, the only victim here is the many people you have hurt. Die black bitch! Eloise, come inside, yard call is over. Linda. I remember when you turned me in because you didn't want to go to prison. Somebody please help me! I am being buried alive and I can't f-----g breathe, nightmares every night all night long, crying myself to sleep. Momma, why was I such a hated child? What happened? The dead can't talk . . . well, not to me anyway.

May 24th 1994. The day began as usual. I was finding myself reaching out to God more. Life really doesn't make a lot of sense to me, never has. Today I had an interview with a member of the Department of Corrections. I was told the reason I was selected was for participation in the parenting group, which turned into a therapy session, and she wasn't even a therapist, just running that fucking mouth. Sitting there with her legs crossed and the battery begins. She asked why was I in the group and I began to tell her about the wrong that I had done to my children, especially my son Tony, and now he and I are worlds apart. She didn't hear a word I said, she was too ready with her diagnosis. I told her upon my release I was involved in a unhealthy relationship, and as I think it over had I given Tony what he was desperately seeking, the love of his mother, things would be better. I mentioned somewhere earlier that I'd left him at the age of two-and–a-half. He was reared in his grandmother's house. Tony didn't live with me when I first went home, but when he did come he became very unhappy. I lived very far from his normal surroundings. I never spent quality time with him. I never allowed him the chance to know me. I was so wrapped up with Norman everything else became secondary, yes, including Tony. As I watched him mature into a young man, I felt old, and my life was so calculated. Work, clean, pay bills. Then it would start again. She spoke and so matter-of-factly, telling me the wrong that I did. Hell, I already know that! Her word was law, point blank, all black and white, no grey. She has become a part of the corrupt system of corrections until she may as well be here with me. She talks criminal just like me But she did raise some very important issues: once I am gone across the river, what will I leave behind for a legacy. Not only have I scarred the three, but then to leave them with not even a decent memory? How much more damage could I do to them? As she talked and looked off the tip of her nose as if she smelled a foul odor, the tears inside rolled down my face. She didn't know the whole story because I didn't tell it. Maybe she didn't want to know, but she sat high on the judgment seat, telling me I should have done this and I should have done that and did I realize that I may have been the reason that their father was on drugs? That was the straw that broke the camel's back, the camel being me. Now, I had endured about as much of her as I could. I interrupted and said for her to just sign my pass; this interview was over. But hours later, I am still thinking about what she said. It's so easy to tell someone what you think that they may need to do, when you are out listening in. I lived in that house and even I didn't know what to do after a while. I thought that I was doing the right things, making sure my children had a roof over their heads and that their environment was clean and conducive to progress, and that they had food and clothes, etc. No, I didn't give Tony the quality time, because I had to work. It's not an excuse; it's a fact. I just read an article about the parole board. It left me devastated. See, this is my crutch, this book that I am writing. It's my pillar of hope. Looking at the words gives me reason to continue on, and I believe that one day I will read it again and I will be free. Smoking cigarettes back to back, I can't put one down before I have another one lit. Things are totally fucked up when you don't have anyone that cares about you. And I don't. It's not an overabundance of self-pity; it's just like that. I can't see the forest for the trees. I can't see the tunnel's end. There is no light. The war that is raging inside of my head and heart leaves me speechless. Have you ever been rendered speechless? Then you know what I am feeling. My release date is in 2005. It's only 1994. We're talking eleven more years! Whew! Truthfully, I don't know which way to turn. I am going in circles inside myself.

At this present moment, I don't know what to think or feel. The situation here is below human.

What I mean by that is the women here, most of them, have given up on themselves and on the hope of freedom, so they participate in whatever will relieve them of their misery and pain. I am jogging around the yard and to my left in the midst of a crowd there are two females in public with others to shield them getting it on. To my right, there is one hitting this girl because she dissed her by socializing with people who had not been accepted by her boy. Oh yeah, you will serve in one capacity or the other: bitch or boy. Now the stud role has its advantages, like the stud can call shots and if he is hot, he really can call shots. I think that I mentioned that before, but he cannot ever show the bitch in him, not even during period time, and he must always look completely boyish, never ever feminine. Sometimes that is a hard task, especially if you have kids and you receive visits. See, you must go visit in your boy attire, and sometimes children don't understand. I don't feel like going through that again. It takes you actually psyching yourself to pull it off right. There is the possibility that you play the game so long you are the game, and that's your sentence for life, and believe me, *it's* hard trying to be someone that you are not. It's hard enough trying to learn who the hell you are. The stakes are high, and it's like selling your soul for nothing, because you don't handle money. It's placed on your books, and really the only advantage is you get to go to the store once a week and pass your list through the window with a false sense of pride for your mate. You feel as if you really are about something and perhaps a little bit better than the have-nots. In reality, you are no more than a commissary hoe. And they expect you to perform at will. Also, you must show up every time to meals, yard call, church class, whatever. If you are allowed to come out of the dorm, you had better step to it. Whatever your peeps are going through, you will also know that's a given. It's amazing the things that we tell ourselves to survive. That comes from whatever we have had to survive with in the world, wouldn't you say? Another note. They are sending them because they will not believe that I'm not in the loop this time. Maybe they are right, and maybe I am only playing games with Eloise, as I always do. Could it be that somewhere inside, I have accepted this life as my life. Hell, look at the years so far. And if I stay the complete sentence, it will be twenty-seven years in *all. Who* the *f—k* am I fooling? I just know that there has to be more to life than this. Count time; all inmates stand to your door; no movement or conversation during count! Now that's a major write-up, disrupting count. Your ass must lie down for that one. You must go to lockdown, do not pass go, do not collect 200 dollars, keeyaw. Two officers will come and count behind each other. Now how hard is it to count single bodies? Sometimes it takes hours to clear, and no one gives a rat's ass if it takes the whole shift. Stay put. *Someone* blaring into a mike to talk to you, saying the same thing, day in and day out. This is how it goes, 24/7, lights on at 5:30 a.m., early appointments and you'd better not be late to them: the clinic or whatever. Breakfast call, you line up and march to the dining hall. Stay to the right of the walk. If you pass a staff member, it's by your leave, ma'am or sir. If you have something to say, you must say permission to speak. Ten minutes to eat, no talking in the dining room. On your way back from eating, if you smoke, you must stop, and you have no longer than two minutes and you must return to your dorm until yard call. During the day, if it is the summer, then it's called when the sun is at its highest, or if its winter then, when it's very cold. What the hell this is prison? I am not supposed to enjoy it, and I don't. Some of the staff enjoy hurting us and humiliating us by doing things like shaking us down anywhere, any time. And like when there is a freak officer present when they strip search us: Take them drawers off; open your legs; now spread that ass wide enough that I can see what you had for your last meal. Forget it, if you have about a nickel's worth of sense, your ass is through. We do your thinking. You gave up that and all other rights. We didn't send for you; you came looking for us, so just shut up and relax. Officer there is a bug in these greens. So push it to the side you have ten minutes and we are out of here, so if you don't have money or no hoe you push the roach to the side and eat the rest, point blank.

Nothing is solid but God. I find myself reaching out to him more and more. Every door to hope is slowly closing, and the other one is cracking. In the natural life, I am through. It's over; the fat lady is about to sing and it's not a pretty tune. In my heart, everyday reality is pushing its way through. I am beginning not to look at the kids' picture anymore. I can't handle this, so now my natural emotions are beginning to numb out, so I try to play games with God. How sick I am. I have begun to talk to others, but my real self is slowly dying. This world is not real and it will hurt you in the long run. I only allow in that which I don't feel will destroy me. I deal just enough to get by. No one really cares in this environment. It's all about survival of the fittest. Maybe one day it will all be over. Inside I'm so hollow, like a tree with no roots. I know that the things I write are lifeless; so am I. I am inside this deep grave, and I can't breathe. But I am alive. I am pulling out locks of hair screaming please! Yes, I was born dead. Why couldn't I have remained so. What's the point or reason? Now I realize that once I became of age, I must pay for the wrong I have done. But what about just being born? Oh I forgot . . . I must also pay for that. Every day I face the oncoming hours, so weak. They tell me that behind every dark cloud there is a silver lining. I missed mine. Or someone else got it. And then they tell you it's always darkest before the breaking of the dawn: let there be light! In this little white room, my life is a living hell. But there is hope. I've just got to bite the bullet and accept my fate for now, and take it one day at a time. It seems so calculated, my being back here a cruel game I can't seem to win. I wasn't a hustler any more. I traded my and my children's lives for family. I had an opportunity to rat them out and make a move, but I played by the rules, but of whose game? When I hustled, there were rules: If you play you pay and if you fall, handle it. Don't go in the kitchen if you can't cook. It's so hard to accept. What rips the fibers of my heart, piece by piece, is that everyone got a good deal but me and my children. I know this sounds so stupid, but I must write or lose it. My son has closed the curtains on Momma Eloise. My little ones don't know me anyway. My dear husband pulled out before I was even sentenced. Bitch. So dear God. where does this leave me? Somebody answer me. Confused, hurt, lonesome, rejected. So for my sanity's sake, I must pull the plug on the kids. I must survive. This is so hard! They loved me. They didn't know me, but they loved me and needed me. Please, God, not like this; not this way. All my life, all I ever wanted was to be loved and accepted. Teach me to love and I will give it back. I only wanted to be happy. Was that so wrong? I can't resort to this life of homosexuality. It's a life of make-believe; it's not enough to hold on to . Look at my feet. They, like me, are so ugly! My toes are ugly, too. I was never good enough. I was always reminded of how ugly I was. It was always beautiful Linda, never ugly Eloise. When I was a little *girl,* I would steal her pretty dolls because I wanted her to like me. I never received dolls, but she did. What the *f—k* , I didn't like them anyway. She would comb my hair so hard, and she would not let me wear her pretty sweaters. She said that I needed a bath. She didn't care for me when we were younger, but as we got older, she started to care. As I look back, everyone that has entered my life has brought some *f---ed* up shit with *him or her*. It's a wonder it took me this long to close the door. Now come on, Eloise, you are no angel. How many times must I remind you of that. I will be so happy when you stop all this*f-----g* whining and get on with this sentence, because you are going to do it. So get on with it .You're talking about what everyone has done to you. . . but what the *f--k* have you done to countless others? When you were the big dick, all was well. But now all the odds are against your black ass. Now you can't seem to feel sorry enough for your sorry ass. Yes, you did have a hard time as a child, but look at what you did when you weren't a child! You are not the only person that wasn't loved, nor will you be the last. And you keep talking about how Norman treated you. If the truth be told, you were more man than he was. And that's how you carry yourself, so don't bitch up now, brother. What about the time you and the rest of them beat a drunken woman all night long for calling you all fast bitches? You didn't forget that did you, sugar? I am you and I will never ever let you forget that I hate you, *as* everyone else does. Yes, I do remember that night in Harris homes. We were bored and reckless and had a point to prove. Never thought about it, but I never forgot it either. Yes, I was very disrespectful toward my parents. Stole from them, never did what they asked. Everything I wanted I just took, and didn't allow anyone to stand in my way. *An*d as long as I was behind the hammer of a gun, I owned the world. Too many memories, and bad ones at that.

♦♦♦

May 28th 1994

I know that I am losing my mind. No matter what I try to think of, my mind goes back to my three children. This morning, after a night of tossing and turning, no sleep, bad dreams, I tried to capture some inner peace. None to be found. I have dreams of my baby girl being raped, and she cries out for me. My son looks out the door for me and I am not there. In my dreams, I go home, and sometimes I can even smell them. I often wake up in the night because I hear them calling me. I can't watch movies that have children in them; it kills a part of me. People bore me. I am attracted to myself and to God, at least that's what I want to believe. Why does she keep writing these notes? I am finally accepting and realizing that my strength and power is but a façade. You know, as if nothing bothers me, when in reality, everything does. Will I ever be able to trust? When and if I do, I pray it will last a lifetime. But I know that it will not be easy to another to enter the realm of my being. The wall that keeps others out also keeps me in. What do I want of another? What am I willing to give? Who am I? What am I about? It's painfully obvious where I have been, but where am I going is the ultimate question. W hat are the facts of my life; what about me, physically, do I like? What about myself dislikes: the darkness of my eyes; they reveal so much more than I would like them to. Do I feel attractive? Why hell no. I don't hold many illusions in regard to myself. Am I a jealous type person? No, because there is neither need, nor justification. I don't have a need for another's person's husband or wife. Hell, those are your troubles. I have enough of my own.

Let me share this: Norman let me know, without a doubt, that when I came into his life, he allowed me there because he had a need. No, not a need to love me, but he saw a potential fool and he cashed in on it. What I mean is, he started with a line as lame as schoolboy's, but without the flowers. Posing as a friend. People know how to do this when they are quite used to misusing people. He said what I wanted and needed to hear and he continued, and even when the abuse was in full force, he continued with the ruthless and tormenting amputation of my spirit,, all the way to the altar. Hell ,why not? What about when I first met Norman? He thought I was hot. He would never put me on the bus. Instead, he walked places with me. He was so proud to have me swinging on his arm! I mean, if we were someplace and another man would look my way . . . oh, he became so upset! And there have been times when he would even say something to the looker. That was all part of a well-planned scheme to reel me into his needy web of abuse. Then the time came when I was huge with child, and he despised the sight of me. Instead of looking my way, he would look at videos of beautiful girls. I truly didn't know what to do with those new emotions he was displaying. I tried not to get in his sight, so he could not see the desperation in my eyes. I needed his love to survive this, but that was the furthest thing from his mind.

What happened to my beauty? I had never before even given it a second thought, because my father had convinced me that I was the ugliest m-----f--ker he ever saw. He told me that often.

Oh, Norman, why couldn't you just leave well enough alone? You were good at what you did. *You convinced me.* I could have sworn that I saw love in your eyes once, but maybe that was what I wanted to see, huh? What about how you treated my precious son when he was small . . . that time you hit him so hard he ran screaming to the front of the apartment where I was cooking, and I got a knife and you ran into the room and locked the door. I stabbed at the door and you called the police, I would have killed you, nigger, had not it been for the police. And why did you try to molest poor Ashley. She was only thirteen years old! Tony couldn't understand how I remained with you after I knew the truth; I know that I have mental setbacks; perhaps that was one of the reasons.

Tony, I didn't want him anywhere near you or your brother or sister. I didn't trust him . . . .No, not at all. That's why I wouldn't allow you to go places with him. I was stuck with this man, not knowing how to get you out. You thought I just didn't love you. Well, fellow, you were dead-ass wrong. I adore you. But as you said, that is water under the bridge . . . right?

Norman, what about that time with you and Toni as I watched from the cold ground, pregnant with Boo. I can't began to describe the feelings that ran through me when I saw you smile at her, and you so gently kissed her lips for what seemed like an eternity. I haven't seen you smile so hard in years, and it tore at my soul. Why couldn't it be me. What happened? You begged me to have you a son. Oh, I get it. Barefoot and pregnant, to keep me in your iron grasp. You sorry-ass bastard! It's sorry motherfuckers like can I? I'll write again soon; larceny is overruling *logic. You* that cause women to end up on death row. I was cursed with loving you. I honestly loved you, *t*he best that I knew how; but what the hell did I know about how to love? I never had the right training for that. I lost something that day in that parking lot, and it was replaced by a monster. I dare not talk about that anymore. Maybe I am better off in prison. I would have come back, anyway. I sure can't tell a scoundrel from a gent, *can I?*

Tomorrow is Boo's birthday. May 29th. Happy *B*irthday, Boo. I never even got a chance to speak to you. I spoke to your grandmother, days before, and begged for the chance to say Happy Birthday to you on the phone. She said that it would be arranged, but it wasn't. Her husband is very sick. I hear that he is losing his sight. I should have listened to him I went to New York to that funeral and Norman treated me poorly. I was pregnant with you, and Mr. Bernard told me to leave there and never look back, because your father wasn't worth shit. I did leave and drove back to Georgia. No, I'm wrong . . . I wasn't pregnant. I had had you and I brought you back with me. I drove all night and he showed up a couple days later. Mr. B. can't give himself insulin any more. It's a lot on your grandmother; maybe she forgot.

♦♦♦

I have my concerns whether the kids are being cared for the right way. They are with Norman, not her, so I must turn it over to God. Norman wasn't the one that looked after them; it was me. I made provisions for their care. If it were up to him, they would have been in foster care. I am told that Boo is a fighter. He was such a sweet baby. What happened? He's only three years old; why so much hostility? When I left, he smiled all the time. He was so playful . . . sucked that thumb, didn't seem to like his daddy at all. Norman would whip him and I got so mad we would fight. I'm here, they are there, and I can't bear the thought of what's happening to my children. My dreams let me know that something is badly wrong. No one in my family offered to help with them. With things the way that they are, I don't know when or if I will ever see them again. Bitch, that's your fault. Yeah, something is wrong. It's the same way they did you when you were a kid; that's exactly what is happening. It's your fault; you should have left him. Do what you always do. It's almost yard call. Run, but I will be here when it's over. After I hung up the phone, I ran long and hard, forcing my legs to go faster and faster. Unconscious of how long I*'ve been running*, tension stiffening my neck. *I can't breathe . . . sweating . . .the salt is mingling with the tears. "Are you a*ll right*? Y*ou're in the recovery ward in the clinic, you shouldn't run like that in the heat." Those pictures again those voices, stop please.

I remember Norman asked *me* for a divorce. *W*asn't it just a little while ago you came to my office at the *S*alvation *A*rmy, all out of breath stars of love in your eyes *like* another minute would have been t*o*o long *to wait.* "*I*t's your lunch break, Eloise, let's go downtown and get married. *W*e already have the blood test. I want to marry you and we will be together forever. *C*ome on! I feel pains in my chest. I will die for sure of a broken heart." I said yes to *your* request, but I will not give up my parental rights to my babies, ever. I never gave them up for Tony, nor will I for the babies. Sure, you can have the divorce. That's the best news I have heard in my entire life. One of life's wrongs that corrected itself. I am so deep in troubles it will take an act of God to help me. They say he looks out for old folks and fools like me. Eloise, you are truly pathetic. I know. I believe somewhere inside that some good will come of this and I will be once again with my children, that's my belief. I have to hold onto that, or just say fuck it all. I am still waiting on guidelines, but that's not all. I'm truthfully waiting on an act *of* God. I have no one to turn to, yet I do have him, always. I'll end.

♦♦♦

May 30th

I am so locked in*!* *C*an anyone hear the desperation, the anguish? Pain . . . so much mental pain. I can't come out*;* yo*u* can't come in. Smoking, my mind stays in overdrive . . . can't stop thinking . . . no one to lean on except those who are already heavy in their own misery. Reason, what is reason? Somewhere I must have seen. I posses the power to reason. But I'm so complicated inside I can't seem to reason. Isolation, deep depression, there she is again, that little girl sitting on that shelf, way deep in that maze, she never stops crying Please little girl, stop crying. Your mommy will come to protect you . . .one day. God, what's the message? What's the lesson? When will this tormenting saga reach its end? How will I meet the final chapter? I could just lose my mind, or has it already left me? Was it ever here? I am alive, breathing, wishing, hoping, praying. I am walking into this damp, dark tunnel and people are reaching out to me. There is Linda, saying turn around Eloise it's not your turn, turn around go back. Linda it's so good to see you. Run, run, run, and try to escape the reality of it all. Please, just a little compassion maybe? Even a drop? Did you show any compassion? Leave me alone! Bad choices, nerves vibrating inside, trying to convince the dear system, the Department of Pardons and Paroles that the last sentence was my breaking point, that it beat all the thrill seeking out of me and that I am more than willing to live life on life's terms. The DA was so determined to end my life, she had herself so involved and dead set to crucify me, and she succeeded. Why wasn't I given the death sentence? You were. *It's* called living death. What's this another trial? Eloise, how do you plead to the charge of being a hopeless menace to this fine society?

Guilty as charged, sir. Didn't I pay my taxes? Did I live on welfare? I worked every day! Inside there is a great turbulence—obstacles to hurdle, screams of injustice, am I not a citizen of these United States? Wasn't I due equal protection? Not even a trial by jury of my peers. No, just the signing of statements because I had a felony record . The ultimate plea bargain, the first to squeal gets the deal. Oh, justice is a game show now. Why didn't someone let me know that all you have to do is rob a store, and since you are kin to an ex-robber place the blame there. Who cares? You all are poor niggers and we need to close this case, so if you all say she knew, it's her case. Keeyaw! Twelve years of mental anguish. I All I know is I received a call from Brenda and she said that Angel needed Pampers, so I left my home one Sunday morning and never returned. Day in day out, can't clear my mind of it. Why won't you let me speak to my son or daughter? What did they ever do but be birthed by me. Man is vile, so corrupt, incapable of administering justice, to be poor and black will always be a crime. My brain is busting; my heart is numb; my dreams are a continuation of my mental anguish. Give yourself a break, Eloise, no one else will, so please give yourself a break. The babies, Tony. Norman, how could you be so ruthless? Didn't I allow you to come back home after your many nights smoking crack? Weren't you there when they ripped my belly apart and reached inside me to get my son? You were not there for my girl. Didn't you say that it was a beautiful thing when a person gives himself to another? You're such a liar. Don't you remember when Special B was born and my wounds began to come apart. I still attended your needs. Did you forget how I worked so hard to make sure that we had a beautiful home? Did you just overlook how I had to be so patient with you when you became so jealous of the baby? I'm being rejected like a bitch dog, like I deserve all this pain. Didn't I pull all the weight, paying all the bills? Why did you sorry motherfuckers do me this way? Take the breath that you gave me, stop this heart from beating, just give me that ultimate peace, would you just do that, Father? Why must I be the one to understand and be so willing to forgive? They fucked me for no just cause. I am having a system breakdown. Who the fuck cares, anyway? The bastard lied. He knew that when I came into that store I was alone and agreed to leave the bags I had. That's who the judge listened to, and he lied. My God, how did it come to this? Norman doesn't deserve my babies; he has never done anything for them; it was me. Tony why do you hate me so . . . because I wouldn't let you run wild? Fuck you, too. Matter of fact, fuck you all.

♦♦♦

June 23rd

Since the last time I wrote in this book, so many things have happened. My counselor make it possible for me to talk to my children. I had a nervous breakdown, When I spoke to the kids, Norman said everything they told him to; he was so empty. I am out of the picture, and I don't have much rope to hold onto. What about this enormous hole inside. I miss my babies so much, I practice daily trying to remain positive and hopeful, but sometimes it's hard. I try to write, but I don't have the strength. I have always been strong willed, but not now. If someone had just offered me a helping hand . . . I can't live this down.

♦♦♦

July 5th 1994

Today Lady y received word that her grandfather died. This is my co-defendant, my niece, my sister's baby girl. Yes, there is a constant war deep inside me when it comes to her. Deep wounds that crush me inside, but still, I can't stand to see the pain in her eyes. The night this happened was the beginning of my end. Now my hard head, my entire being has been destroyed. If I ever had a chance, I have blown it. The final results have left me emotionally drained. I've lost three beautiful children, not knowing if I will ever see them again, I am sorry for your loss but it only reminds me more of my own. Received my guidelines. I must serve ten of these twelve years. I just served ten, about three years ago. Whew! No one cared enough to consider my babies. My son Tony would not offer me a hand with his baby sister or brother, so I had to send them over two thousand miles away. I still have milk in my breasts for my baby; she is only seven months old. My sister's health isn't good, but I do love her, though not her children. I must have been a bad person.

♦♦♦

July 10th 1974. . .

She lay on that old sofa. The night before, I'd heard the death roll. It was a sound that I cannot describe. My mother was sitting in the chair and I was going to comb her beautiful hair. It was early in the morning and she didn't curse or call me a dike or spit snuff on me. She just sat there, and I asked her a question, but she never answered. I never heard her voice again. Momma, I miss you! There was so much I needed to say. Everything has gone so wrong everything, Momma! Not that it was ever right. If I am ever freed again, I will build me a new life—alone. I don't know if God has taken his hand off me, but I do know that I have ruined and wasted my entire life. Not giving a damn how the game is played, this bitch said something she should not, and as it goes, it's either her or me. The last two years have been crazy. I went back where I said I would not go. I have several girls to see about my needs. No more begging to make it from one day to the next; no more pain. Just get aboard and ride to where? Who knows? I met this girl and her father has some pull. They want her away from me, so guess what? I'm on my way to Metro State Prison. That's how it goes if they want your ass gone. Look for that early morning wake up when everyone else is asleep. Get up; pack your shit; it's time to relocate.

♦♦♦

August 7th 1996 . . .

I seem to have lost years somewhere. Back when I wrote often, I had hope of freedom. Then I received my papers. I just didn't give a damn, so I turned to what I knew, the survival tactics I was used to. They were waiting with open arms. I closed my heart and fell right in line.

As I ride up this highway, I think how a few years ago this was my home and I was happy. Cut. No more reminiscing. Life goes on. No room for emotions. Only the strong will survive. Come on, let's go to this camp and lay it down, like only you know how to do. Keeyaw.

Now this is a drab looking joint and the girls all seem medicated. Everyone is placed in the gym for intake and to learn where they will live while here. Eloise Greene, J1. So here I go. Now what awaits me there as the door opens to the dorm? There is a host of women, all white except for a few, standing looking at me like I have stepped on sacred ground. I was placed in a dorm with some celebrities. This older woman is using the toilet and she looks up and sees me coming in and forgets to wipe. She just shakes the pee off. Whatever. Move, bitch, this shit is heavy. What the fuck are they staring at; I glance into the tin mirror to see what's wrong. I still look the same. That's your bed, one girl says. Yeah, okay, thanks. Do you want me to help you put your things away? I can handle it, but you can wash that locker down with bleach. Now, if they are this nice, there is something amiss— like she wants me. The old broad comes back and says its lunch time, so I stop unpacking and line up, but up here these women got it going on; they don't have to line up. So we stroll on out. Why is it that this these women are the original Jane Does and they get the VIP treatment and only special prisoners are permitted in their company and the old broad I come to find out is none other than Stay the Night herself. Boy is she feisty and talks more shit than I do. As the days pass, she notices that I don't jump at people's beck and call, nor do I eat pussy.

They had this warden wrapped around their hand, and they got anything their hearts desired, and Ms. Stay the Night had had a boy, but she ran circles around him. She thought that since when the doors closed and the lights went out, I was in her room, perhaps she might want her clit licked. Oh, no, honey. Wrong one. So I was invited closer so that maybe she could satisfy her curiosity about me. I would sit and chat and then they gave her her own room and her mate was on medication, so one night she sent for me. I must admit, I was equally curious about her, since everyone told me that she didn't do black girls. I set out to prove them wrong. One night, as we sat on her bed, she asked a millions stupid questions and received equally stupid answers. She was just wasting time. It was the weekend, and we could stay up later. She said, "Are you afraid to come and sit on my bed?" I said no. "Then come and sit," she said, so I did and she touched my arm and I did the same, but I am a little more seasoned at foreplay than she was, I could tell. I reached over and pulled her face close to mine and told her, “Make your move.” She opened her mouth for a kiss, and I kissed her so passionately she had to grasp for air. She wanted me to do it again, so I did. She tried to guide my hand between her legs. I politely got up and went to my room and got in bed. She could not understand that. She thought that I should have been hyped about her. Bitch, please give me a break. So the next day at the print shop, she's hot for my rudeness the night before and she tells her boy that I made a move on her. So this nigger comes like she might be going to kick my ass or something . She walks right up to my face and says “ Check this out; she is my gal and you are not to ever say anything to her again.” I spit in the bitch's face and said, “You are never ever to speak to me without first saying permission to speak . . . *got* that?”

It seemed as if the entire print shop came to a halt and since Stay the Night ran things, she told her boy to just calm down, that she would handle it. Had it been *anyone* else, she would have had them moved out of the dorm, but she wanted a piece of me. But she had to wait her turn because the serial killer who lived in there had made her move and knew how to handle her mouth. I would listen to her because this girl was smart; she was a nurse and knew how to kill. She often said that she didn't mean to do what she did; she just felt sorry for the older people that lived there. She was kind and very used to treating her folks right, but her money wasn't quite long enough, so I had to hold back the love. I wasn't permitted to make love to her, so I let her have her way, and she made love to me as often as I would allow. Sometimes I was awakened to some hot lips, and if I slept on my stomach my ass was parted and licked. Umm, I liked that. I had to coach her to get me off. I told her to very gently caress my body and never to rush, and to gently rub my breasts, and then suck them until I couldn't stand it, then move on down and tease my inner thigh, and then smell me. Open up my lips and open me up until you see that tiny hole and place your tongue as far as it can go inside and stay there. In and out. Then get my clit and suck it, kinda ruff but with perfection, and when I say I am about to cum, slide back down and get it, then get the fuck off me so I can go shower. And I will call for you; don't come on your own. If I were to develop any feelings, I would have her watch someone else make love to me, and I would have someone make love to her and watch. That's how I killed any emotions. The word got around and Stay the Night wanted some action, so one night she calls me in her room and she gets me to finger her. Naturally, she wants what the others can't seem to get— my head. That will never happen, but I got hers. *There* was this girl who swore she was a Muslim and would never ever give herself to a woman. Whew, was she the freak, and gave excellent head also. She rode that pole good, too. I had knocked off over half of the dorm when the word got back to admin, and I was once again shipped to another camp. I would be sent back later on to Pulaski.

Now, these girls had plenty of class, and I liked that. It was a different joint altogether. I began to write plays for the prison, and I really enjoyed that. I met this one female who was so special and I really did like her. I never did do black girls because they always wanted to fall in love and would clown on you anywhere, but the white girls really were smoother. They would lead you to believe that they cared, but they only wanted playmates. *Liza* taught me that, and yes, I learn fast and good. I began taking pictures for the coach, and I really did like her; she was nice.

There was this service called *K*arois. It was about agape love and it was on a weekend that I was forced to come back to my senses. I was asked to participate in putting all my hate for anyone in the sea of forgetfulness. I tried it, but the hate was bigger than me, and I had masked it with prison life.

I was called up to the office and told by some officers, laughing, that my sister had passed. I had talked to her just a few days before, and now I was told she is gone. Linda was a very nice person toward me after we got grown, and she was right by my side throughout my life. She never judged me, though she would tell me when I was wrong. But she was a friend. Now I don't have Linda. She's gone. They didn't even place a stone on her grave. Yes, she had her faults, and for years she was an addict, but time changed her. I could depend on Linda for some of my needs in prison, and she was a friend. Now *Liza* was back and I told her about Linda. She cried; she knew her well. Things were not the same for *Liza* and me. She was married to Jack and he had her on a tight rope. When she had gotten out, she had hooked up with Makita, and they went crazy. Broke into the DA's house. Damn, girl, have you finally lost your mind? I knew about it before she came back because I'd read about it in the paper. I no longer loved her, not as before, but as a friend for real . But she had this notion that every time she came to prison, I needed to stop whatever I was doing and just pick back up where we left off.

As I jogged around the pavilion and I sweated, the sweat would turn to white salt on my skin. This very smart lady, who was a nurse, said that it shouldn't do that, so I went to the clinic on sick call. They asked if I had other problems and I said no. I was so *worried they* had me sent to Atlanta for a test. They gave me a shot and it made me dizzy, but I could tell what they were doing. They put a tube up my ass and one down my throat and told me everything was fine. For some *reason* I had more test, but they found a spot on my right adrenal gland so they removed it. The doctor who did the surgery told me he had never done that type of procedure before. He cut my stomach wide open, and I had what seemed like over seventy stitches and I could not walk for days.

One day, I was permitted to go to the pavilion to walk. On my way back to where I lived, I saw a fight in the yard. It was a friend of mine, Gee, and another woman, and they were getting it on good, so an officer came . Mr. Handley was directing the women back to their dorms, and where they were fighting was a hole, so with all the women standing around he really couldn't see. I didn't want Gee to go to lockdown, so I slowly went to the fight and tried to grab her, but she was swift on her feet and got past me. I was holding my stomach so I wouldn't get hurt. As I was straightening up, here came the officer. Everyone was gathered around the fight, so when he went in to stop it, they started to kick him because he was so big and he was laying on Gee, and she was popular. As they attacked him, I was trying to tell her to please let him put the cuffs on her, but she wouldn't. He had to use force. By now, other officers had arrived. One officer from another dorm said she had seen me hit him. That was a lie. Now everything went bad. I was given a free world charge and placed in the hole, in the shape that I was in. After about a year of going back and forth to court ,I received this letter from my public defender:

> December 3rd 1999, RE: State vs. Greene. Charge : Aggravated Assault; Battery. Dear Ms. Greene: As you have been previously told, your case is scheduled to be tried the week of December 20th-24th. Because there has been so much conflicting testimony among your witnesses as well as the witnesses for the state , the Chief Assistant District Attorney, James Turk ,is offering the following : If you pass a polygraph (lie detector)test while asserting your defense, the State will dismiss the charges against you.

> However, if you assert your defense and fail the test, the results of that test will be used against you in any trial of the case. Of course, the decision is completely up to you.

This happened in July of 1998, and I had received so much hell over this from the staff that I said yes, I would take the test. I was given a lie detector by the GBI and I passed it, so the charges were dropped. God knows I was tired and needed to be free; but life for me inside didn't get any better. Although the officer himself said that I hadn't kicked him, by now it was personal. The staff felt the test wasn't good enough, so every way I turned, I was defending myself for *something*. They rode me like a bucking bronco. They had no problem setting someone up, so I had to be on the lookout for razors being placed in my shoes. They were the only personal items left out. I met a girl, one of several. She was African American and smart as hell. She and I got together when I moved to E-5. She became a very special person to me. She was not only my lover, *but also* my friend. She would look out for me any way that she could. She would sometimes bring baloney in her bra from breakfast when I didn't go to eat, which was often. I learned to survive off a cup of soup and Cheetos. It kept me from starving. I grew to love her. She didn't know much about this life. She just liked me. She really didn't know anything about women, and it tickled me when she tried to learn. After awhile she went home. She left me a diamond ring that will remain with me always, to remind me of her. If I ever got to go home, I would give her this ring back; that was our pact.

I have created some enemies on the staff. The warden instituted a procedure called a staffing, in which we can air our grievances against individual staff members. I have to take coach to one. She called me a black bitch, and yes, I will take her to a staffing. Another officer is a redneck. He can't stand me. Why? Because I always write plays and I am quite active here in prison. I told him that my boots were too tight, but he made me wear them anyway. I will also take him to the staffing. The warden allows these staffings because she knows how the staff is; she has been in this game long enough to know when some shit is in the deal. I thank her for that. This warden has been in the system as long as I have, but she is fair.

I won the staffing. I mean, the truth prevailed.

I wanted to be transferred from here. I got my wish to go back to Metro, but things had changed and so had the warden. Now there is this man who says we prisoners are not fit to kill. Now every day we must take the wellness walk. No matter what shape a person's in, she will walk for one hour. There is no more Jane Doe dorm, nor does any one prisoner run the joint. So its fifty-fifty, every man for himself, and God for us all. Now, to go to sick call you must pay a fee. Come on now, we're in prison! It doesn't matter; you pay. Something else they added is the cert team. They are like the swat team on the streets. They come in the dorms and shout shake us down, and they tear our rooms apart looking for items from outside. Hell, we can't get to campers or cell phones, but that's what they are searching for, and colored panties. Okay, now that sounds like prison yesterday. Now the women are going through a new thing. Most of them are on meds and are doing crazy things, like killing themselves. The staff are shooting them with stun guns, putting them in caged rooms, or on the floor with death row inmates. They are hanging themselves and all sorts of shit. Staff is still getting down with inmates, still getting fired. Time for another transfer. *Liza* is a pain in the ass. She wants me and I don't want her, so she tells me that no one will have me while she is here. I ignore her, so she hits me with a damn trashcan over my head and thinks that I'm not going to break her neck. Wrong. I threw her down some stairs. It wasn't but four steps and she is all right, but with this warden, my black ass has to ride back to Pulaski—back to the rednecks. Eloise Greene all the way, before the dawn breaks, away with you . All right, Greene, you know the ropes. Let's do it, they say in ID, so I put my game face on. By now I have a reputation that precedes me, and everyone knows Greene but herself. Whatever it takes to get the job done. But inside I am so tired and weary. I want to go home, wherever that is. It has been years, and I am growing tired.

Didn't take any shit whatsoever from staff or inmates. To deal with the staff, I would study what rights I did have and meet them in a staffing. *The inmates* We would just get it on, fighting or *f-----g*, their choice. After the staffing with the coach, I was placed on ground maintenance, and the officer that was over it is more than I care to write about. If I was right, then why was I being placed in the notorious heat? Two reasons: *First,* the situation with that officer, when I proved that it was cruel and unusual the way I was forced to wear those boots that were too narrow; then the staffing with coach and all the others that I had called. Yes, they had the last say.

No visits from the children and there's hardly ever any mail. I was tired after the last sentence. If I can just hold out a little while longer, run more, start back praying, I'll pull through. I don't like this life, but I must struggle on.

I met this girl—kind and beautiful, but a little heavy. Still, she's okay. We've become very close and she has this officer in her pocket, so we can spend some time together. But she is a turn out, and doesn't know anything. I am not about turning anyone out to this sick-ass game, so the time I spend with her is platonic. But she is listening to these other women and just has to try it, so I gave her the test: I asked her if she would allow me to see her with another woman, telling her that I would really get into that. She went for the bait, and as far as I am concerned she belongs to the one that turned her out. It brings to mind once back at the beginning of my sentence. I met a very beautiful young lady and she and I became close. One night, she was ready, and so was I, but something just didn't feel right. When we went into her room and she immediately cut the lights off, that sparked my suspicion, and I asked why she had done that. As much shit as she talked, why be bashful? So I got her to undress, kissing her passionately. As soon as her clothes hit the floor, I cut that light back on, and to my horror, her pubic area hadn't finished developing. Yes, her top was developed, but I could tell she wasn't much more than a teen. I asked her to please tell me how old she was. The truth, please. She was upset and she cursed. "What difference does it make?" she said. I said, "Just tell me the truth." Seventeen! Now, that wasn't my style at all. I got the hell out of that room. She was mad as hell, but I didn't give a damn. I know how it feels to have your innocence taken, and I wasn't about to do the same to her. After her fury died down and she allowed me to tell her why I had reacted as I did, we became the very best of friends, and it lasted. Of course, I later found out she did get an older woman to turn her out, and when I found out, I was furious, because the female had HIV, and she knew it. But then I found out that she only gave her some brains, so she didn't catch it.

Well, it's time to be transferred again. Why? Because the counselor found out about that night's episode. And this girl's father has money, and he wants her away from me, so I'm on the road again, back to Washington State Prison. Back through ID where they will take items that I can't have. I am really tired of prison life; God knows that I am. Time goes by, doing the same thing day in, day out. There is a problem with spiders biting the women. Two women died from it. To get the heat off the prison, they put out an article that said *it was* not spider bites but staph infections *that killed them.* Whatever.

I did see my kids after about seven years inside; they were afraid of me and didn't know me. I never saw them again, while I was in prison. I did receive a letter from Norman, Jr., written on May 12, 2004. It said:

> Dear Mom,
>
> I love you, but don't like you. Do you know why? Because when I see people on parents' day or bring-your-child-to-work-days, that makes me feel so doggone sad. My friends say my mom this, my mom that, bla,

bla, bla. When someone asks where is your mom, I always say she is away or she died. But I do hate *you* that you stay out of my life, you stupid woman. You have been gone so damn long I barely even know your name. But I am good; I am in the seventh grade doing very well. You should know that. Do you know why? Because you should be here and not behind bars. Just never come here. I am doing perfect with my grandma. Well, my dad is locked up, too. You did not know that.

Sincerely, Norman, your son.
(Did you know that?)

Whew! Now that tore my heart to pieces. I didn't ever hear from the kids, either one of them, and I can understand why. But why couldn't someone have cared enough for them not to allow them to hate their mother. I can understand the grandmothers not wanting them to have any love for me because I wasn't there, but what about them? Why weren't they given a choice in the matter? Both the grandmothers hated me, so they took it out on the kids. Neither one of the fathers contributed any positive input. Both are lifelong crack users, so really, they haven't fared much better than I have.

I am supposed to get out next year, if I make parole. I am up for it now, so I will just continue this routine. It has been ten . . . almost eleven years. It's almost over, and my plans are to get a job and save up so I can go to New York and once again be with my children. For five years after I got this sentence, every night I cried myself to sleep, I ran *every day*, and I did cross the line from sanity to insanity, but by the grace of God I came back across. I applied myself and I went to school and took classes for my problems—such as anger, management, parenting, and so forth, and learned skilled trades, learning how to forgive myself and others, reviving hope and the possibility of a normal life. In any positive course they offered, I was present. Now, I wait my turn to be free. That sounded so strange to me. *"Eloise Greene, you must go to the mailroom. You have legal mail."* I often felt that I would never make it but now it is on the horizon. Yes, it's here! "Eloise Greene, after careful consideration, the Board of Pardons and Paroles has decided to depart from your *guidelines*, and you are to continue to expiration, two more years." That's because of that shit with that officer. I may have passed the test, but I lost the battle.

Back to the yard. I am angry, but I must continue on somehow. Seconds turn to minutes; minutes turn to hours; and hours turn to days turn to months. A while back, I received a letter from one of my nieces, and she borrowed the last money I had to my name. She promised to pay it back, but *it*'s been almost two years and she still hasn't .

Who really cares? No one! I hold onto this writing, because it gives me time to think. It doesn't matter about the money, because I will go to a halfway house pre-release, so I can get a job and make some money and go and begin a new life. Finally, the time has come, and they are calling my name to be transferred again. This time it's to the halfway house. *In Pursuit of freedom.*

Thank you, Father, thank you *truly your grace has brought me a mighty long way your grace and mercy has been sufficient and have allowed people in the prison ministry to come and minister to us caring when they could have been doing other things*. I will make myself a new life. I am here at the halfway *house* and even the air smells different. The sky is so beautiful! Clothes . . . . I can put on clothes! I can use the phone and eat decent food, but this place is very cutthroat. These women will do whatever it takes to remain here. Back on guard. Finally, I get to go to work. I land a job at this restaurant, Piccadilly, and they pay almost five forty an hour. I don't care; it's a job and they like to hire women from the halfway house. We will be dependable because we will do whatever is necessary to remain on these *jobs*. Finally it's freedom *time! January 23, 2005, happy birthday Eloise*

I am about to be free! I will pick up my check and I am out of here. Is this it? Two hundred dollars? I don't have a place to live. I am going to New York and this is January and I don't have a heavy coat. Please don't take what little money I have. I am sorry, but the rest of the money goes to rent here at the center. I can't believe what's happening.

♦♦♦

After twelve long, hard years, my first night free is spent in a bus station, and I am scared to death. As I sit here, there is so much running through my mind— a million questions. I think back to the time I was in prison, at the beginning of the sentence. I didn't know how I would ever survive. I met women who to this day are so dear to me and always will be—they are the family that I never had. There are women in prison who would definitely be an asset to this world. I mean, if you are not famous or not of worldly importance, then you are like I am, just another person of no significance. Well, when a community of those types of people get together, they create what is needed to survive, and the really good part is you can be who you are, because there is no opportunity to be a phony. You are together 24/7 and there is no way your game is that tight as to deceive one another. Prison doesn't offer privacy, not even bathroom time. I felt safe there. I don't feel real safe now.

I remember when I first went to the halfway house and I had to ride the train. Jesus Christ, when those train doors flew open and those people gushed out, I nearly fainted. So many people, and they all seemed in a rush. I felt so out of touch with things that I had become accustomed to: like for the last twelve years, eighty-five percent of the guards were female. There were a few male guards maybe, but now to be in men's company made me nervous. The looks on their faces in prison . . . I learned a little about the faces and body language and kindness in the eyes. The women I left behind, I would find a way to help, but first I needed to learn to help myself.

Computers are what's in, I must learn to use them. I don't even know how to turn one on. My children . . . what are they like? I can't wait to see them. For years I have followed them daily in my mind's eye. I wish that I had seen them more. I wish that I had made better choices. Why did it happen this way? Calm down, Eloise, you are going into overdrive. I will be happy when the daylight comes. That's strange. . . . I never feared the night before, but that was when I didn't know fear. I do now. These people . . . some appear to be living in this bus station. Please, God, I don't want to lose hope. It's daylight; I must find some place to bathe and I must go to work. I have to get the money to get myself on a bus to my children. When I left, there weren't so many people on the streets. I must also find a place to sleep where I am safe.

At this job, the customers are mostly gay males, and I swear they are so beautiful to look at! No one would believe this. They are so pretty and so kind to me. No judgments from me; I have been judged all my life. I don't look for your faults; I can't see past my own, so it's okay by me to be who you are. A few more checks and I can go. When I talk to *my* children on the phone, they sound as if they would like to meet me. There is a God! I think I am about to be, for once, a happy woman. I will work real hard there and try to build a life and a relationship with them. I don't have anything nice to give them, nothing but a heart full of love. That has to be a nice gift. I'll bet they are beautiful! I can't wait!

I had a friend in prison, and she gave me a beautiful diamond ring. Well, I saw her today, and she is going to help me get a place to stay for a while. See, that's what I'm talking about—the bond that was created in prison is still strong. What would I have done if she didn't happen by? She gave me money to get some food, and this place is so nice. It is a room, and it is clean and pleasant. She never asked to be repaid, nor did she spare me any kindness. She is available, and I will remain true to our friendship—always. She got me some clothes and will help me get a warm coat and the money to get to my children. I found my other friend's numb*er in my belonging* . I called, and she said, "Sit still; I'm on my way!"

The first night I stayed here, it scared me. This huge bed! In prison, I became accustomed to a bed so small a child would find it difficult not to fall out. Here I have a bathroom that I do not have to share, and a bathtub. The only bathtubs in prison are in the clinic. And I have a microwave and real silverware. It was plastic there. I could, if I choose, put the television on and watch it from this bed. It's nice. The beds in prison were made of steel. This one has a boxspring that's really comfortable, and there's a refrigerator. My God, I must be in heaven! It's night again and my heart is beating so loud I can hear it as I lie on this pillow. I haven't been totally alone at night, and I am afraid. I have been behind a thick steel door with a deadbolt lock, where a guard made rounds every hour, in a steel building, behind fences laced with barbed wire, to keep me in and others out. This night, I missed that protection. Here only that one door protects me. . .

I must have dozed off. It's morning and I am excited and happy. I have found two of my old friends and I have a nice safe place to lay my head . . . and just everything! They both called this morning to make sure I was all right. I spoke with my daughter last night and she seems really excited and can't wait to meet me. She's seen me only once, years ago.

I must learn where to catch the bus . . . but more important, I must remember how to get back here. I came back to this town and it's totally strange to me. I don't know to catch the bus to my job . . . oh my God, what if I can't find that place? *It's* out of the routine that I was used to . . . Let me go to this lady in this boot*h*. "Excuse me, please, where do I catch the bus to Anstey Mall?" She gives me the directions. I left early, so I have time.

"Can you give me some change ? I need food."

"Here, take this ."

"Thank you. God bless you."

Inside my mind, I say, *N*o*,* my friend may G*od* bless you. They advised us in the halfway house not to give to the street people. They say it will only be used for drugs. I say if a person will allow himself to stand on corners and beg, then that's humiliating enough, so let it be between him and God what he uses the money for. If I have it, I give it. I have come to know how easy it is for people who have none. They've gone through different trials in life. It's easy for them to conclude this and that, but sometimes there is truth to what they say. Yes, of course, sometimes they are playing games, but like I say, let it rest between them and God.

♦♦♦

I am at work, and these are some fine people. Perhaps if I were a dude, I would give some of them some rhythm. I know how it feels to be different and to be treated less than human. I long to see my sister's children, to make sure they are all right. No, they didn't make any effort on my behalf, but I still have love inside of me for them, no matter what. So I brave up and call my niece, the one who was involved in this last crime. She is excited to hear from me, and I ask if I can come to visit. I will go this weekend. There was a time that whenever I thought of her, my anger burned, it was so pain-filled. Now, I only pray that she is all right, and that my other niece is also. And I want to see my niece who's sick. I have a number where I can call my oldest son, too. Now I am really excited! He stopped writing and I lost contact, but I will call this number.

I told him I was in town. He asked me where. I told him. I prayed that he would want to see me.

I am back at the room and my fingers shake as I dial the number. It's ringing. "Hello," a voice says. It's a male. I say, "Hello, may I speak to Tony? He *says, "This* is *he, "and* then silence. I *say,* "Hey, this is Eloise, your mother." Silence for what *seems* an eternity.

Finally he *speaks*. "Who?" he asks. I repeat. "Eloise. . .your mother."

"How are you?" he says, and for a *moment,* I hear joy, but only for a fleeting moment. I say, "How are you?" And he says fine. I tell him I'm in town and would like to see him. "Where are you?" he asks," and I detect that fleeting note of joy again. He *says, "I* will be over today, okay?" I'm so excited I drop the phone. "You will?"

He *says,* "*Yes*," *and* I say, "Okay, please come." I am real nervous now and I can't sit still, so the hours drag by. Finally, a knock on the door. I just look at the door for a moment, *hesitating,* for two reasons: First . . . hell, I am not use*d* to having a door; second, I'm not used to answering one. It's been a while. Will he accept me? I ask, "who is it" and peep into the door.

♦♦♦

My God, it was him! I had waited so long for this! On the other side of this door was a piece of the great hole inside of my soul. I opened the door and the most handsome men was standing there. About six-foot-three and slim, with eyes just like my own. I couldn't hold back the tears. There was so much that I needed to say. I had said it over and over for twelve years, but now I was speechless. He said, "Can I come in?" I felt stupid. "Of course you can." Please, won't you come into my heart also? I could tell that he had trained his heart not to show his emotions. The reason I recognized it so fast is that I have practiced it for years myself. For self-protection. It is what I call an ever-present gatekeeper. I needed it as a child and as a reckless teen. It protected me as a prisoner, and it helped me keep my focus so that I didn't slip too far away into a fantasy world. When it has been a part of you for so long, you can't easily let it go. And just as it protects you by walling you off from hurt, it harms you by holding you apart from those who would love you. We talked, and I saw that there was a girl with him. He introduced her as his best friend. He wanted me to get dressed and come ride with them to see one of his children, and I agreed. I didn't care that it was late and I had to go to work the next day; that night, I was where I wanted to be—in his company. I rode in the back seat, happy because I could stare at him without him seeing and becoming uncomfortable. We finally got to the place, and I didn't know what to expect. This may sound wrong, but at that moment, I wanted to see his child more than that I wanted to spend time with my own child, one that my heart has longed for so long. Maybe it was because I could see that he had no intention of getting emotionally involved.

♦♦♦

I knew what I'd seen when I first opened that door. On the way there, he told me that the mother was named Ally, and to approach with caution. That caused me a moment of thought. Anyway, we went in and the home appeared unkempt. To me, that was the first sign of problems, because no one wants the ones they love to live in filth. This was our first time meeting. My God, she was as old as me! That was another sign. What did she want with such a young man? Perhaps just a young lay. But anyone could look into his eyes and see signs of emotion. His son was called from the back or wherever he'd been. I believe that was his son. He had features like Tony's, but I could also tell something was emotionally wrong with him. I could see it in his eyes. As we rode back to my room, I commented that the boy looked a lot like Tony, and I asked a few questions, not wanting to say what I really was thinking or ask the questions that I really wanted to ask. We arrived at the room and said our good nights. I could see that I had never entered into his heart. Maybe he'd just wanted to see me since it had been so long, out of curiosity.

♦♦♦

The next day found me deep in thought about my son. It was almost the weekend, and I was to see my niece. I had my friend take me to her place, because I sure couldn't have found it on my own. As we approached her stairs, something was stirring inside me. It was the anticipation of joy. I knocked on her door, and she opened it quickly. Again, I could not hold back the floodgates, and the tears flowed. Once, before all that had happened and before the baby, she had loved me, but as I looked deep into her pretty eyes, I saw suspicion. She invited me in, and there, inside, was her daughter, who is beautiful and so very well mannered. My niece was expecting a baby and soon to deliver, so as we reminisced, I was careful not to stray too far into the past, and we soft-peddled through that part. Her home was very neat and clean; that was a great sign. And she appeared to love her child enough to be rearing her right. I adore that in a mother. So as the evening continued, I had another surprise: my other niece came by. I was really happy, because she and I hadn't spoken in a long time. She appeared to be happy to see me, but after the visit I realized that neither had offered me a place to live until I could do better. I decided to look beyond all that. I was now free and we could work to make it right.

The time came when they asked if I wanted to see my brother-in-law. I said no. God would have to work on me a little while longer before I would be ready for that. I had expected much more from him. And forgive me, but I always see him in that room saying we are all going state.

♦♦♦

I went back to my room and sat down to think about the visits I'd had with my son and the others. If only I didn't know what I had seen, it would have been grand. While I was there, I asked about the baby. One lady had been keeping her after Linda died, but now some other lady was keeping her. When I thought of Linda, it broke my heart. I now had enough money to get that one-way ticket. So I bought myself a coat, and I was on my way. My friend had given me a DVD player to listen to as I traveled. I didn't know how to use the thing, but I figured it out. I had never been so excited in my whole life.

♦♦♦

I traveled in and out of different bus stations. At first, I was afraid to leave the bus because I was afraid it would leave me. So many choices of food! Boy! But I was too excited to eat.

♦♦♦

Look at the *beauty; I* cannot believe it! I have always marveled at how creative God is, how perfect the colors are, and how beautiful the sky. We are now coming into snow. Now look at that beauty! But it is falling so hard it's scary. Calm down, imagination, you will arrive safe. I envision the bus going off a cliff and I might never make my destination. I will make it! They want me to make i*t*. Just a few more hours. Finally! We are here and I can't wait! I don't know what my son looks like, but I am sure we will recognize each other. Looking around, I see no one here for me. Didn't I tell them what time the bus would arrive? I may have been too excited. Where is the number? I have got to look through all this junk to find it. Everything that I own in this world is here with me, so I have to protect it. It has been hours. I can't reach anyone on the phone. This is not a good sign. Finally, after almost five hours, I look up and one of the most handsome young men I've ever seen is approaching me. He says, " I just had to see you. I have wondered for years what you would look like. As he spoke, I was in a daze. My Boonan is a big boy now, and as handsome as I knew he would be. His eyes are friendly and questioning, but I see human compassion and mercy in them . . . and caution. I wonder . . . . Here is his grandmother. Now, she is a great pretender. She will have you to think that her kind words are sincere, but maybe not. So I don't ask any questions about the delay. I am happy, but there is a strange feeling brewing inside.

♦♦♦

We entered their home, and it was very unclean, and you know by now to me that is a bad sign. Anyway, there was growing tension. It was getting thick. Then one day my ex, their father, showed up, and all hell broke loose. The first thing he did was choke me and call me a sorry motherfucker. I grabbed his hand from around my neck, not wanting to do this in front of my son, but he was the one to take his father's hands from around my neck, breaking my heart for a fleeting moment. I could have killed the man.

My plans had been to stay and make a life there, but every day it became crystal clear that wasn't what anyone else wanted. I was still living in this fantasy that it would be fine; I ignored anything else. The grandmother constantly complained about me cleaning. I needed for her to want me around, but it wasn't to be so. I made the decision to go on back to Georgia, and my son said that would be the best thing. I can't describe the pain. The rejection was more than I was equipped to bear at that time—so much, too fast. I hadn't been out of prison ninety days, so it was too much, too soon. As I was preparing to leave, my intention wasn't to go to my daughter who was living with her aunt. I had spoken with her on the phone she said she didn't want to get to know me. My light of hope was growing dim, but the aunt spoke to me and told me to stop by and see my daughter. She was only seven months when we parted, and I had only seen her once since then. So with a heavy and dejected heart, I got on the bus to go where she was living. I was told to catch a cab and come to the house, and so I did. When I arrived, the aunt came to the door and helped me with my bags. She said that my daughter wasn't home from school and that she hadn't told her I was coming. I don't know if that was a good idea or why she chose to do it that way. I often wondered if my daughter had been treated poorly. For some reason, I knew that there was a difference in the way my children were being treated. The grandmother favored boys; that's all she'd had. Why would you surprise a child like this. It was a bit much.

♦♦♦

That evening when she arrived, I was sprung on her, and she didn't like it—not one bit. I could tell that something was seriously wrong. I could also tell that she was just like me, and that was scary. She was icy cold and mean. Her aunt had to tell her to be kind to me. I was told to sleep in the room with her. She said no way. So I slept on the floor in the front room, and I had to be up before everyone else so I could get my pallet up. I tried everything, but nothing worked. By now, my soul was dying.

The aunt asked me did I want a boyfriend. I thought, Now what do I need with a boyfriend? I don't have eye water left to cry, I am over twenty-five hundred miles from what I once called home, just getting out of prison with no means of supporting children who don't want me. What the fuck do I need with a man? I don't know what to do or where to turn.

♦♦♦

My friends call every day and I tell them everything because it just doesn't make since to me. The aunt has ideas of me remaining and living in her basement— down there with those cats. I don't think so. So *every day* I endure my daughter's agony. She is so confused and a manipulator. What has this child gone through? The aunt drinks like a fish, and she reminds me of my father. She doesn't like my son and really doesn't like my daughter, so now it's time for a visit from her brother. It's a holiday, so he comes and I must watch the difference she makes in how she treats my children, but I can't say anything; they don't like me. Anyway, it's a nice day and I have sold my rings. I don't have any money and I dare not ask them for any, so I give the children money to go and get goodies from the store. They come back with a bag of sweets and they don't share them with Norman. He gets mad and I know that he sees me standing in the door, but it doesn't matter. He lets out a string of profanity that would put a grown man to shame. He shows no regard for me whatsoever, and I ask him did he not see me. He looks at me like so fucking what. He turns and continues to curse, so I take the broom and hit him. He says for me never to ever hit him and the look in his eyes was one of hatred. He tells me that the mother and son thing will not work.

♦♦♦

One day, my daughter was having problems and she was instructed by her aunt to take this medicine. She decided that no, she wasn't going to, and told me to do whatever I had to but she wasn't taking anything. I gave her a whipping and she hated me more. So I had to leave there after only three short months. I'd had such high hopes for my life, and I just knew it would all be fine, but I was so wrong, so defeated. I decided that I couldn't take the rejection. Just as I was making plans to leave, the aunt said that her rent money had gone missing and blamed me, so there was insult added to injury. Like a whipped pup, I was taken to the bus station and sent back to Georgia. The ride was so long and cold; the outside matched my heart—cold and grey.

I had no plans, no place to live. I called one of my friends and she said that I could come and live at her house. They were kind to me and treated me like family, but I wanted to learn how to take care of myself, so I called the Department of Corrections and asked if there was a place that I could live near the city so that I could find work. This was a small town. The search matched me with a woman who had me to pay four hundred dollars a month for rent, and I didn't even have a job. She had me call different agencies for assistance. I searched for work and solicited agencies and churches. I couldn't get any more help, so I had to leave her house. I went back to the small town. I had spent almost nine months searching. I went to the Labor Department and they would send me to apply for jobs that didn't hire convicted felons. What a roller coaster ride! Finally a commissioner in the department who cared started a program called "Take Five Felons and Give Them a Job." I had filled out an application for one company and I told them the truth about my past. They said they would call me, which they did. Praise God Almighty.

I don't care what it takes, I will keep this job! I am living with my old friend, whom I mentioned sometime back. She has been that a good friend. I think back to prison; there were times that as I jogged around the grounds, my mind would spur me on to believe that somewhere I would actually have a life, and I would once again be reunited with my children, and they would love me as I do them. We would work and get a home. I have never had a home, so I often envisioned this really nice place, and from different books and magazines, I would build this home on the inside.

Let me invite you inside my mental home. There is a long driveway made of beautiful earth colored brick, not hard looking, but friendly, so a person will not be afraid to enter. There are a few steps to the entrance, and just outside is a pair of small cherubs; that's to represent that God lives here, and they are here to protect us. They are smiling. Come on in; step in to the foyer and look to your right. There is an umbrella stand, and to your left is a coat rack. Look down and the gleaming tile stairs shine up at you; step inside this beautiful room to your right, which boasts a lovely wall of shelves lined with books from everywhere, about everyone, excluding no one. There is a comfortable sofa and its matching chair and a chaise, and there is a fireplace large enough to sit in front of with the family, to have a quiet time and just chill. They will tell me of their career plans and seek my advice. I don't know what portraits will hang here. We will decide. There on the floor is a colorful area rug. Let's go even further. Now we are in the dining area. Look at that table and those chairs—the finest oak. There isn't much furniture, but some. Now, let's step into the kitchen and look at the cabinets, the countertop, the stove, and dishwasher. But I will mostly do the dishes myself. The sink and the island—earth colors all around. Let's go straight up these few stairs. To your right is the bedroom that my daughter designed herself. She doesn't want anyone in there, so let's pass it by. There are four more bedrooms designed by the occupants. I can share my bedroom with you—I don't mind. There are hardwood floors, a wingback chair, and a small table in front of the window, and fresh flowers in a vase. A nice window with flowing drapes, and a balcony for privacy. I have a sitting room for myself with windows and entertainment unit. There is a stand-up cabinet in my bedroom, and a four poster king-size bed, a nightstand, and a clock. In the sitting room there is a phone. I can look out of my window and see the back yard and the flicker of the crystal clear water in the pool. I can see comfortable lounge chairs and the serving tray and the fence for privacy. I can see the landscape, the well-manicured lawn, and the colorful flowers—azaleas, forsythia, and spring tulips in all colors. And look, there is my handsome dog, a husky with blue eyes and a grey and white coat: beauty untold. Every day he and I run through the woods and stop when we can't go on, and I lay my head on his beautiful coat where we stop to rest by a peaceful stream and I whisper how happy I am. I listen to the soft water splash against the rocks, and look up at the sky and wonder what God is up to. I touch the earth and sit up and take in all this beauty, and whisper a prayer: thank you. I will think of using that spare room I have for one of the ladies who is just getting out and needs a helping hand.

♦♦♦

Back to reality now. It is almost time for me to go to bed so I can be well rested for orientation tomorrow. I can feel happiness on the horizon. Maybe when I get working, I can really have a home and a nice one. And maybe the kids will not hate me so much and will want to come and live with me and get to know me, and they will not be ashamed of me as they are now.

I didn't really say what I felt in New York, but each day as I went to apply for jobs and assistance, a part of me inside was dying from the rejection of my family. Perhaps it was meant to be this way. The grandmother had to put her life on hold so that she could raise my kids and she was the type that still had life in her. I learned that her husband didn't like kids, so I really don't know what to think. Dealing with my daughter and seeing how mean she is, I just don't think she's fared much better than I did in the love department. She is so defensive and wants love so badly, but rejects mine. Will someone help me with this one? But today I have been given a second chance on life and responsibility; I can give prison credit for quite a few things as to my betterment. It taught me patience and it allowed me to see the reality of a given situation. And it taught me survival.

I must go to sleep so that I can be fresh in the morning. Just think, I can get my own place, because no matter how nice a person is, they tire of seeing about a grown person, no matter what the situation . I want to pull my own weight. I must also get a car. It's morning and I didn't dream. I dream all the time and the dreams seem so real.

She will drop me off and pick me *up. There* are quite a few of us here today. I have only been out nine months, and I really don't know a lot about being free. But I sure am going to try. The meeting begins, and the first thing I notice is that everyone is white. Not that it's a problem to me, but my friend was briefing me on how it goes, and unfortunately, there is a problem with the color of a person's skin. I don't care; that's their problem. We are told that there is to be no joining a union. Cool, I hadn't planned on joining one anyway. They offer a health and fitness center. Come on, man, now you are talking my language! They give us coffee and biscuits from Chick Fil-A that's really nice, and lunch will be served. We will have a week of this and still get paid. That's good; I need it. I will give her money for living in her home. I receive food S-tamps and I give those to her also, but that will end. They are giving us all the pertinent details. After this week, we begin work. I must train for a week on days and then go to nights—seven to seven, twelve-hour shifts. I don't care if it's fifteen-hour shifts.

♦♦♦

First day on the job and this woman who has been here twenty years is training me. She is nice enough, but there is another employee who works with her who is very territorial about this woman, as if I might become her friend, so she is always mean, mugging me. I come to learn why she reacted that way. I cannot explain how good it feels to have a job, and this appears to be a good company—strict. It reminds me a lot of prison, but it's not.

I have gotten in touch with Chap, and she wants me to speak to some women in the prison. Since being freed, I have become a member of the Alpha and Omega group for women who are coming out. We are to help them re-adjust, and I work with some women I was incarcerated with. We get together once a month and go to different churches to try and get help for our organization. We speak and have dinners. I like that, and they are happy that I finally found work, but it was the commissioner who really helped. That's all the more reason that no matter what, I must endure.

I can't tell anyone at work anything about myself, because this company doesn't hire felons, and it would hurt to tell. Yet, this is a small town where everyone knows everyone, and too much silence is worse than talking too much. So I stay to myself and work. I know that this is a white person's world here inside the *factory*, but it doesn't matter. I am no longer training and they can't seem to decide what shift I will go on. *the J shift* is mostly blacks, and the *G* shift is mostly whites. *J* it is, and I am thankful. On-the-job training and it is very hot in here: no air and plenty of work. I start off as a *blocker* of *damage* or scrap *cloth. You* are not allowed out of your work- place, and you have breaks: two *ten*-minute breaks and a *twenty-nine* - minute lunch break, and you must make production. This company owns this town, and you must do what you are told or you are out. There is a *seven*-month probation period, and you can be fired for anything during that time; I mean anything. So I am on time and I work very hard to please, and pray that they don't fire me. I stay to myself.

♦♦♦

After the seven months, you *a*re allowed apply for another job if it should come available, so when a area job became available, I applied. I had never even seen a lift, let alone driven one, so here is where my troubles began. I was given a trainer who didn't know much more about lifts than I did and he knew even less about training another person. He was a hick and a redneck. He didn't like blacks, but that's the majority of the factory. I expressed a desire to be an operator, not a lift driver, and there's a difference. His reply was all they want around here is for you to get the job done and that's it. Matters continued to get out of hand and I had nowhere to turn except to the factory manager for his advice. He was the type of person who would listen and do what was right. This was in the early part of 2007.

My hire date was September 19, 2005, and in between, I had gotten myself an apartment and registered for school so I could upgrade my skills, of which I had none in computers. I began school in 2006. My friends say that my apartment's a dump, but it's a start. The only items I had were a green suitcase, which was a gift, and its contents. I moved in and got my electricity turned on. I had no credit, so I had to use alternate routes for everything. That's no problem though; in time, I will get furniture and everything else I need, but for now, a roof over my head is fine. Like anyone else just getting started, I bought just what I needed—a bed, a shower curtain, and some small things.

♦♦♦

At the school, *north* Central Tech, the instructors, like most in this town, are not very friendly, and they make me feel as if it is a shame to be my age and know so little. I can't speak about why I am lacking so much, because that would mean I would have to tell the truth about who I am and where I came from, and that would be the talk of this small town. So I continue on.

The commissioner has requested that I speak at a luncheon. I am so nervous! The owner of Angel Food Ministry is here, and countless others. I have

Chap here, so at least I know someone. It's my turn; Chap has introduced me. My legs are shaking so badly I might need a cane to stand.

Hello, everyone. *My* name is Eloise, and I am so honored to speak to you concerning the program, Take Five, which was initiated by the commissioner himself. I was released in January of 2005, and not until September did I land employment. Being an ex-felon and living by society's rules, finding employment is almost *impossible*, because no one wants to hire an ex-felon. Had it not been for the intervention of Take Five, I don't know where I would be. Thank you.

♦♦♦

My mouth was getting drier by the second. As I looked at the audience and my words ceased, my mind went into overdrive, and I wondered if there would ever be a chance to live this record down. With a record, you can't get a decent place to live. So, what are we to do, and does anyone really care? In prison, you don't have to scheme, manipulate, or plan the downfall of another, because the groundwork is already laid. I mean that the only time those things are done is when you get written up and mislay the truth of the matter, or when there is someone that has something that you want and that's the only way you can get it. Prison is cut and dry, every day your routine is the same, except when you change the rules, but that never lasts. Prison is a place for change and getting it right; it's a time of reckoning and getting real, accepting the truth, and finding out who you are and how to play by society's rules, because no matter what they are, they are already in place and non-negotiable. I have learned that change must benefit, not destroy, and I have also accepted this truth: I don't know all the answers and never will. I have accepted the hard fact that yes, I was cheated out of the most precious time of my life, the beginning, and I, Eloise, did the rest. I should never ever have borne children, but God knows all. I often mention God, because there is no one else. I often look back over my life, and I am amazed that one person could have destroyed so much. My anger was larger than me, and I knew mental pain and anguish. I was often confused at how people treat one another. I received all the wrong messages. The scales of my life were unbalanced. I knew hate before love, lies before loyalty, mistrust before trust, savageness before integrity. God intervened in ways that I cannot fully explain. Just recently, I had a wonderful opportunity to look into the eyes of a child, and I saw there the light of hope. Her eyes were dazzled with fascination and wonder as she looked upon the beauty of a statue. I saw how the stars in her eyes sparkled with a beauty so pure and deep that I cried. Someday, she will be whatever she chooses, not what has been chosen for her. Her mother had love for her and protected her and allowed her curiosity to grow, her innocence intact, not molested, not left with unbearable shame, with no one to turn to. I hope she will not have to beg or sell her soul for someone to really love her, and that when she makes mistakes, someone will care enough to explain about choices and consequences, and what is right and wrong. I often wonder this: Where is my place in the Bible? Why so much pain, just for being born with dark skin, an African American? The rules that were in place for my people—was it part of a master plan to mentally destroy us, as a people? What wrong did we do to be treated this way? So many unanswerable questions! I do see the will to survive and conquer. That will lives inside of me, and I know that only God will nourish it to live on. We all have obstacles and always will have them. It's not what has happened to me, but how I respond and how I choose to fight, and try to be a light in some one's dark tunnel. Since my release, it has been one mountain after the other. First it was homelessness, then no job, no food, no family— but still every day, my strength was renewed. I can't say why my drive is so strong; every corner I turn I face rejection. Sure, I have been rejected my entire life, yet it's a feeling I just can't seem to get used to. Each time it happens, another piece of my heart trembles. When I look into my own eyes, I see pain, desolation, and ruin. I will not allow myself to feel sorry for myself. I will allow my heart to feel victory! Daily I fight depression concerning my children's mental state and just how sorry a mother I was. No one could punish me more than I punish myself over that. On Mother's Day, no one calls, and I live in that isolation. At least in prison I had an excuse. I couldn't receive calls. Each time I become something else. Come inside, if you will. Walk down the dark halls of my mind. No lights please. You don't want to see in the light. Gatekeeper, please allow them entry. Yes, come deep inside, for that's where I live. Inside of this carved hole is my home. It's cold and damp and lonely. My only visitors are my constant pain and my memories. We must leave now; I can't tarry here for long. I am too afraid I will stay. No, I must come back to life.

♦♦♦

Today is Mother's Day. I have given birth—no, I was cut open like an animal so that hands could be placed inside of me to withdraw a child. My body was unable to give birth the normal way. Perhaps that was a sign that I should never have had a child. Who knows? Three times this has happened, and such beautiful babies, so pretty, so healthy, and my God, so full of life! Damn you, Eloise. Tony, Norman, Brionna . . . Today my heart grieves for them. *Please, one* of you just, call. I have a side in this tragic saga. Does even one of you wish to hear it? Not one of the three has any association with me, as if I were a leper. There was a storm last night. The thunder clapped, the lightning flashed across the sky, the wind howled, and the trees bent under its fierce pressure, a tornado warning in the area , an eerie silence about. These are the exact feelings in my heart and head. If I should live until tomorrow, I will be once again reminded of my failure and my destruction of humans *who* deserved so much more. Crashing limbs and brokenness, just like that between me and mine. That awful silence between us.

God, I have never known peace. Don't *let that* happen to *my children*, please. Look at the hate and anger in Brionna's eyes, because I wasn't there. Yes, I often wonder what they went through while I was away. I'm sure that their hearts hurt also, because each of them is so very bitter when it comes to me. It's been like this every year since they were born. The tears are falling just like the rain outside. There is no electricity, sirens are blaring, and airplanes are flying overhead. The night has passed. Birds are chirping in their language, perhaps saying happy Mother's Day, too. In this apartment, there are only outside sounds, and there is only the light of day. What if there were no light at all? *Would that* be an excuse for fucking up people lives? This pathetic life of mine . . . who cares? Has all life's happiness passed me by? There was none . . . I don't remember. The many years spent in prison, always looking forward to reuniting with my children; please don't slam that door shut . . . please. When I looked into *your* eyes, I *see* only contempt, hate, and a strange pain. *You* are unforgiving and unwilling to try. Death is looking real good, but *you* may need me. Hey, I can't penetrate this thick fortress that you've built. You must know that I did the same toward my parents, and my life has been a living hell. Please don't make my mistakes! Rise above your hurt and pain and frustrations and hate for me. In order to live your lives, you each must forgive. That's the only way. God will make sure that I get my just due for the wrong that I have done to each one of you. Don't try to do God's job; it's too big for you. Every move that I have made toward you all since I have been free has been wrong in your sight, but I know that you can't live in this world and not respect others, and I know that it would be so wrong for me to sit by and watch you self-destruct. Norman, the day you stood there and cursed like a grown man over candy was wrong. Even if you were not taught to respect me, you should have been taught to respect yourself, to respect an adult, and not to speak such filth. It may have been wrong of me to hit you . . . but I did. For that, I am sorry. And Brionna, when you folded your arms and said, "*D*o what you have to do," try to understand that was not the way to handle the situation, on your part or on mine. But you must remember, I had been there for a while, and you were out of control. The time you allowed your cousin to sit in the bathroom with you as you used the toilet—now, that was a lack of self-respect. I don't care how close the two of you were. I hate incest and anything that reeks of it. After being in the company of each one of you, I was shocked at how you were being reared. You all were being set up to fail in life. Don't you realize that I have spent a total of twenty-seven years in confinement? I sa*y* that because I was driven by hate, and my payback was self-destruction. History has been known to repeat itself. Not only was I in a physical prison, but a mental one as well. God's intervention has allowed me true freedom. This has *just recently* happened. My life is been like a scene in the fable of the *b*eauty and the *b*east, only reversed. I relate to sad words in songs, such as *"I Who Have Nothing."* Even when I had money, I was very, very poor. When there is disharmony in your soul and the very essence of your being is torn apart, you are poor in every aspect of your humanity, and the beast inside will dominate. Head hung low, only hollowness inside, I am about to lose my mind . . . or have I already lost it? Was it ever there in first place?

I returned hopeful that, in time, we all could make the wrong right. A rude awaking is what I got. Hell no, I wasn't stupid enough to think that after a lifetime of no Eloise, like magic it would *all* be made right, but what I did envision was that one of you would have the will to help the others try. It has been three years since I came back. I am confused, and my light of hope is dimming. This has hit like a trillion volts of electricity while I stand in water trying to hold on. Please let me do what my mother couldn't: let me hold you in my arms as I do in my heart, and reassure you that I will leave again only in death. And if I can wait for you on the other side, I will reserve for each one of you a seat. Please know that all the mistakes were mine, and I am so sorry. I do love each one of you with all my heart. There has not been a day since any of you was born that I wasn't mentally with you. You do not have to love me; just forgive me, so you can live. Let me give you the comfort that only a mother can give. The only comfort I had as a child was when I was in Juvenile Hall, away from the rats and the filth and the awful way my father treated my mother. Finally, Mothers' Day is reaching its end.

Tomorrow I must perform as a normal person. Lay your burdens to rest until the next time.

♦♦♦

Learning to operate this *lift* has been pure hell. The people are so damn mean. I must bring pallets and spools to this older woman, and I have others that I must service. She is so mean! She must be sixty- nine or older, and she demands that I come immediately. It's taken me a while to learn how to operate this *lift*. It's such a small area to maneuver in, and I have plenty of stations to get to.

Let's talk about this place. When you enter the building, you can be walking right beside someone and they will not speak. There is a racial divide; only the whites are secure in their employment. Since I have been operating this lift, I have had several problems and at one time, I could go to the factory manager. He was kind. There are a lot of young people that work here, and teens will be teens. They knew that I didn't know how to operate the lift well, so they played games with me as I tried to work: like they would step in front of me, and when I had to move items, they would get behind them and jump out. So I decided to tell the factory manager. This is a letter I wrote to him. It will allow you some insight.

Dear Sir,

I am writing this because you are out of town, I believe. Sir, the reason for this letter is, as I have said to you so many times be-

> fore, *is* about situations *in the factory*. I am not taking up lengthy office time as before, but putting my observations in writing. First and foremost, I would like to express my gratitude for the opportunity to be an employee here. And as I have stated previously, there can be no more humane a person *than* yourself. Without delay, the reason I am writing this letter: Sir, please forgive me for not writing someone else, but we both know you are the only one who cares.

On such *an*d such a date, a *barrel* fell over as I tried to move it. The reason I am mentioning this incident in detail is because I, as always, want you to know the full details. I was written up for this and asked to sign it. This warning stated a weight and footage. I became suspicious of the ticket, so I took another exact *barrel* and weighed it, and it was off. I later discovered that the footage was purposely changed to accommodate the weight that this type *lift* can carry. Please check into this matter. I need my job.

Here are the facts: #1 –The *Tobago lift* #605667 has a weight capacity of 4500 pounds. The *barrel* I attempted to *lift* was 95,000 feet, weighing 4526 pounds, which exceeds the capacity of the *lift*. I saw on the tag *that* the gross weight is 3466 lbs., which is different from the actual weight, and incorrect. I do not know what caused the difference in the weight. My *lift* rules and regulations state on page four that I should never exceed capacity weight. When I *lifted* the *barrel* the rear end of my *area bus* came completely off the floor. I have all the data to support my assertions in this matter. We both know that from my first day on the *area bus* there have been incidents, the first being that my supervisor let me drive without certification. You were very concerned at this and had the matter corrected. Sir, I never went into details over that matter because I didn't want to add to the problems that already existed. I mention this now because you need to have a record of the facts. I have an outline of *my* official duties in writing, and I also have the copies of the actual duties that were assigned to me by my supervisor, knowingly that they were someone else*'s* duties. Now, I mention this because I was told to make sure those duties were done before my own, which caused a delay in completing my own duties. I have been cleaning another department before your morning inspection .You are aware that I was sent to the *factory*l head office because my area wasn't inspection-ready. I have had endless problems with shipping, placing the items on the conveyor, and being subject to insults from the shipping supervisor. They gave me the option to stop operating the *area bus* and go back to the machine. Why am I being treated this way? I asked to please be able to speak to you before I made a decision, as you've known from the beginning there have been problems from persons wandering from behind items *and* stepping in front of *the area bus*. Sir, I can't afford to complain because of the cliques here. I heard the supervisor in shipping make the statement she didn't feel that there should be affirmative action. Now, she has the right to say anything that she pleases, but maybe that's not appropriate for a supervisor to say publicly. What do you think? I don't want her to assist me anymore, because she said that while she's helping me, her department is short-handed. So please, thanks but no thanks.

♦♦♦

I continued driving until I got it correct and operative. I know that I am being done wrong and am doing another's job, but I need this job, so I must endure. No matter what, I am happy because the children are coming for Christmas. I can't contain my joy! Thank you, Father, thank you. Now to hopefully make a better second impression. My oldest son will come down also. It doesn't get much better than this. I must save all my extra money so that I can get them gifts, or I can give them the money and they can get their own gifts. I am just so proud they wanted to come. There is a God! Now, I must get special food. You know, for the holiday. I don't shop because there is no one but me, and I will eat whatever is there.

Back at the job, things are not looking good. I am driving much better and learning to operate the *bus*. First, I had to get over the fear of it. This truck operates from its rear wheels, and it's very convenient. However, it is also very dangerous, and one needs to know how to operate it properly. The young man who was teaching me how stated that I only needed to know how to get the job done. And that may work for him. He has been in the country all of his life, riding cows and dirt bikes and large farm equipment— large tractors and such. Even in prison I wasn't exposed to that, so it is new to me. Last night, as I was making my deliveries to the machine operators, I noticed this man who worked on the *another* shift waving his hands and shouting to a *person* who was on the *machine*, and as I got closer, I could hear the angry words and cruel threats that he told the *person* to relay to his young friend. I heard the last words the angry man said before he strolled off. This company has taken on the task of helping troubled *people* who would not ordinarily finish high school, and has given them the opportunity to earn money and work they are out of school, but they must finish school. When this person first started to work here, he cursed like no young person should, and he stated that he drank and smoked. Because I am older and know first-hand how easy it is to ruin your life when you are young with no guidance, I would try to talk to him every chance I got. He was like any other teenager, and gave the impression that he was Billy Badass, but as I sat on *the bus*, I could see fear in his young eyes. As I got closer, I heard the man say, "You tell that *medical-----f-----g* nigger that if I catch him near my wife, I will string his black ass up and tar and feather him." I could not believe my ears! It wasn't as if he didn't see me standing there as he made his speech. The younger one was shaking and tears welled up in his eyes from fear. When the man walked out of sight, the boy rushed into my arms and cried. The supervisor noticed and came over and asked what was wrong, and he told him, word for word. This was the supervisor's reply: "Oh, he didn't mean it that way." He spoke as if nothing was wrong. No apology for the remarks that were made to the boy or for the racial remarks made for my benefit. I later got the complete story from the floor. This man's wife worked with the *people* and had gotten emotionally attached to this one black boy. She had given him her cell number and he would call her. Often, the husband would check her phone, and he saw a text that was not good. That's why he acted the way he did. It still didn't make it right. It happened again, and he choked her and got fired. Nothing happened to him for coming in on another shift and threatening another person's life. But here, everyone knows everyone, and they are close. Also, this man had worked here for more than twenty years, so that speaks for itself.

Shortly thereafter, the boy was fired. They said it was because he couldn't keep, up but after that happened, everyone had beg*u*n to call him a nigger lover, so we all knew that it was only a matter of time. It appears that it did him more harm than good. I see him every morning when I get off work and he doesn't understand what happened. They had told him that he didn't have to rush to learn, and that enough time would be provided, yet he was fired. After this incident, the same supervisor rode my ass. One time, the *bus* driver in the back got fired, and I had to do his job in addition to mine. One day, after getting cursed out for being late on a pickup from this female's machine because I had been instructed to take care of another job first, I put in a request to be *transferred* to another department. I had to be very careful because I did not want to lose my job over matters out of my control, but after that, I was under another supervisor, which was great. Life was okay for a while.

Back to the visit. . .

It was Christmas, and I was going to pick up the kids. I could hardly wait. I looked up the hallway and for what seemed like an eternity. I heard voices— lots of different voices— and I heard laughter, and as the people poured out. I held my breath with anticipation. Finally, they appeared, and like rays of sunshine, there they were, my reason for living and for putting up with the shit around me. Nothing else mattered at that moment. We got the luggage and decided to go to the International House of Pancakes for breakfast, and the kids finally met their older brother for the first time . I cried—not for me, but for them as they looked at each other. Everyone ate and had a great time, and soon it was time to drive home and listen to stories. I have a niece who has a voice like Whitney Houston's, but younger. She sang happy songs, and my heart was at peace as it had never been. I was part of a family for once, and it was my family. Not the women in prison, but my family. They appeared to be happy. I had never been home for a holiday, nor had I ever decorated a tree outside of prison, so this was all so exciting. We dropped Tony off in Atlanta, and he promised to join us that evening, so I began to cook and had a friend help me. I am lost in a kitchen, but I would watch the families on TV and wanted that warm feeling of preparing a meal. I liked trying, anyway, so we got situated and everyone did their thing. We just sat around for an hour or so, and my older son came back to join us and brought his small army of kids. I wanted to spend this day with my own children, but it had to be shared, and so it was. Tony prepared to give presents to his children, but he had none for me or for his sister or brother—not even a card. That made me sad. His children had paper thrown around and it became a mess, and it only got worse. My son went upstairs and down, cutting hair and not cleaning behind himself. One ugly incident led to the next, and he and I had words. Finally, he spoke from his heart, and said, "You never cared for me, anyway." I could sense violence in the way he carried himself, and I went into my protective mode. I went into the kitchen and got a knife, and I remember the venom in my bitter words: "Boy, I will fuck you up." Words that should have never been said. But emotions were running high on both sides, and his last words were, "You don't have to worry about me ever coming back in your house," and he collected his children. My younger one once again was afraid of me, and she joined him, deciding to stay with her older brother until it was time to return to New York. I regret it to this day, because they never came back. My agony was upon me again. No one to blame; that was on me. I have never known what to do with my emotions once my feelings get hurt. It should never have gone that way. I have always had this belief that my parents allowed me to do whatever I pleased because they didn't give a damn, and I wasn't going to allow this from mine. But I seem to have forgotten that I had never earned their respect or their love. I must have thought that I automatically deserved that. Every fool but me knows that it takes time for a young person to readjust to major changes such as this. Yes, I have always self-destructed; I have always been my own worst enemy. I was never able to separate the times past from future and present. As I think about it more, I have never known how to work things out. I've always just worked with whatever happened. The beautiful tree that we all decorated— me and my children— it shone so bright! The little soldiers and the beautiful stars . . . Oh, my, the bright beautiful lights! I watched as they picked out special ones and gently hung them on the tree. I will take that moment to my grave . . . the hands of my children on Christmas Day! I cried so much I had to go the emergency room.

May I stray for just a moment and allow you into my thoughts? Oftentimes, I ride my bike, and I not only do it for exercise, but to be able to see in person the beauty of life. You know . . . just slow down and maybe pick a wildflower and touch its stem and smell the true essence of its sweetness and look at its perfect colors. I often go to one particular very beautiful place, and there I jog and walk. I look at how evenly the water in the lake moves. Still water runs deep, they say. Yes, it's the dead of winter, and it's as grey as my heart. There has to be some meaning to this madness. I can't seem to get it right. Will

I ever have another opportunity to say I love you to them? It was the look in his eyes that assured me that this time was my last. Once upon a time, I had so much else going on in my head that I would not allow myself feelings of love or passion— anything that I knew would hurt me. I was driven by my pain and anger, and my heart was as strong as a lion's. Something happened over the years, and to this day, I can't say what exactly it was, but it's as if my human feelings have returned.

Back to the madness of the place I work . . .

They say that they are giving me and others another chance, yet I know as well as they do it's all hype, and a chance with a great condition attached.

Let's talk about school some . . . . Now, I didn't have any knowledge of computers, so I went back to school. I was under the impression that school is the place to learn, and I came to realize I should have gone to school at the appropriate time of my life.

Even though I did take classes in prison, right now you'd never know it. Everything is so hard for me to grasp, and the instructors act as if it's a crime to be grown and coming back to school. Everything is taught so fast and the emphasis is on just passing the tests. Don't worry about really learning; just get by. They are so assured of themselves here at *North* Central Tech. They don't even offer tutoring in computer information, but I must remember that this is part of a very prejudiced small town, and so, I am on my own. I wish that I could tell them why I am so slow, but it would be used against me in this small town. My schooling is paid for by the lottery, and I don't want to lose it, so I work twelve hours and go straight to school. I just can't get it as fast as *the* others. They look at me *as if* I am stupid, but I want to learn, so I endure the agony, holding on by the skin of my teeth. That's a familiar story. Maybe next year it will be better.

♦♦♦

I do volunteer work with a group called Alpha and Omega. We go to different churches trying to connect the community with the system. Every person who commits a crime should be punished for the wrong done, but as you have read so far, sometimes prison isn't the answer, and perhaps we need to be proactive in reforming the system. I say this because ultimately everyone will pay for the shortcomings of the current system. How so? It's safe to use myself as an example. I have caused so many innocent taxpayers grief. Every time I broke the law, everyone had to share in paying for my welfare while I was inside. I often say people should stop pointing fingers and help in whatever way they can. To the many innocent people I have harmed, from the depths of my soul, I am more than regretful and ashamed and sorry, and I do ask for your forgiveness. It's Christmas, and as I look into the faces of the inmates here, my heart grieves. I don't know but one way to talk to them, and that's to tell them that whatever they left is still waiting for their return. Life has only moved on, waiting for no one. The rules in society have already been made. We must meet life every day on its terms, as it is, not how we wish it were. It will not be easy, but we are our own responsibility. I mentioned the word shame, and I now realize that the word and the feeling that goes with it will destroy a person who is not careful. I have lived a life of utter shame, and I didn't realize it until of late. So what do you do with your shame? I have accepted it, and I am learning ways to live with it and move on. You know that you are shame-based when every time certain subjects, such as being sexually violated and such come up, you find yourself trying to rearrange the truth. Shame has made me scrub my body almost raw to try and get the filth off. I look deeper into the eyes of these women, and I see so much. I tell them that there are questions—such as *why?*—for which there are no answers, at least not in this life. Yes, there are answers, but not now. I share what I have experienced since I have been free, and I stress everyone must do their part. Life will not respect or tolerate a slacker. They have an opportunity to ask questions, and they often ask if I like my job. I answer that I have bills to pay, and as to whether or not I like my job, at this point it is unimportant. They come back with, shouldn't you like *the* type work you do? I say, "Yes, you should. But I never did the things that I should have done to be able to be choosey. I, like you, have broken society's laws, and have made myself exempt from certain rights." No, I did not directly answer the question, but who is to say that once they are free, their situations won't be better. I do my part in that I kiss ass and do whatever is needed to try and help pave way for them. I have accepted that the Department of Corrections will always be a part of my life. But I like this way better. I have now chosen to be in control of my own life. I want to be the navigator. No more being driven by my pain and my whims. Before long, I know that death will come calling and this pathetic life I have lived will be over. Inside of my heart, there is a desire to leave something of value behind to my children and to mankind.

My children, as I have shared, don't express any desire to know me, and they are ashamed to be mine. Now, let's talk about that. No child should be ashamed of the one who brought them into this world . . . do you agree or disagree? When I was younger, I had shame for my parents . . . great shame. I also had shame for myself, for the many, many lawless acts I committed. When I was in elementary school, my parents never came to any of the events, and so on, and that had a profound impact on me, so I am sure that it has had the same on my children. So many things are brought to the front of my mind about how everything we do in life. . . every decision we make, every action we take . . .has an impact on others. Perhaps that's one of the reasons I enjoy reaching back to my prison family. There are those who do deserve some recognition, because they carry a very important message to the world. Do you agree? I often wonder about the readers of this book. I wonder if they are thinking something along the lines of *What* the hell *is* this*,* just another blah, blah sad ghetto story*?* or *W*ho really cares what you went through as a person? or *d*o you say*,* what I *can* do to make this world a better place for myself and others *who* share it *with me*? Perhaps there are some who share my agony, yet desire to fight for freedom of the self, and really strive to become a better parents or a better people.

I have come to realize that you cannot get away from my kind; we will not just go away; and from what I see today, it's only getting worse. I passed a man the other day and his hat said Vietnam Vet. He was outside of Wal-Mart, and as I approached him, I said hi. He was kind, and said hi back. I asked him if he was really a vet. He told me that he was. I thanked him for protecting me and my country. He smiled and said thanks. As I was about to walk away, he said he was homeless and had traveled on a bike, which was parked by his side, from Florida, and that he had been ripped off. I said, "Let me go to my car and see what's inside, and I will give it to you." So I did. Now world, United States, why? . . . how? . . . what happened? He fought for our safety and for our freedom. He sacrificed his sanity so you could continue to live safely. How could we not protect him better? Surely he deserves that much! As I look even further, I see we as humans have become desensitized to the pain and suffering of others. We can see a child go astray and only point fingers, or try to protect our own from that child. Even I can see that's not the way it should be. Stop and look at how we are going as a people. We must try something new and better to help mankind. When we help others, we are, in the long run, helping ourselves. In the private chambers of your own mind, you know that no one can escape the madness that we, as people, have created on this earth.

Let's look at this. There was a time when African Americans could not just do anything they wanted to, or go anywhere, or live anywhere. They were sequestered into limited areas, limited activities, limited employment, and limited educational opportunities. In certain places, people thought themselves to be safe from crime as long as they were separated from people of color. But today, we live everywhere and go everyplace, right? Compare this situation to that of convicted criminals today. Perhaps the time has come to recognize the rights of those who have paid their debt to society and are trying to start over. Wouldn't it make reasonable sense to try something new? When do we stop pretending that we care and start really caring? The truth always comes back and bites us in the butt.

I know that my writing seems to jump from one subject to another. That's how I think. I don't think on one track, but many tracks just keep popping up, as ideas present themselves.

Don't we know that our turn for disaster will come, and others will turn their heads away from us? Just look at the disaster of Hurricane Katrina. My God, look! And let's not forget the tsunami. Did we do all that we could have to help? Look at 9/11. We still haven't recovered to this day, probably never will. Did we do all we could have for those victims? Or did we make sure that our every act of help was televised and that every good deed was recorded, public, and duly accredited? Have we become a brood of vipers? I was at friend's house recently, and her mother couldn't do enough to make me comfortable in their home, offering me food and drink. Yet when I was a child, this same lady would not allow me in her home because I wasn't a good girl and she did not allow her daughters in my company. She would feed my father, but not me, after my mother passed. I see this all the time—people appearing so holy on the outside, yet in the private chambers of their hearts, they abhor others whom they feel are not in their league. What's there to be said of those actions? Just a different viewpoint to ponder.

♦♦♦

Now this is a new and promising year. Back to the job and school. No glad tidings to be shared over the holidays. Deeper in the emotional hole than before. Like the gambler who has been wiped out, there is no way to pay this debt. Sleeping with a person who doesn't love you, yet you go on, and you ask God to intervene.

Let's talk about computers and the way they have swept us off our feet. And let's not forget cell phones. Now, I can remember a time when we didn't need so many phones. That brings to mind how we create needs for unneeded items. Yet we will not care for those things that are really badly needed. We don't always realize that we already have what we do need, such as other humans. Computers have moved the clock forward. We are giving up so much—mainly our privacy. I have already stated that I don't know jack about computer use. I bought one and got lost, and I had to call India to get help. That's who answered my help call, someone halfway around the world. I gave them permission to repair the damage from their distant computer, and as I watched, they operated mine from theirs. I thought, *Wow now that's something! If they are able to do that,* what else are they able to view? And America, are we not getting too relaxed? We don't have any privacy.

Yes, we are moving forward, but to what? We no longer talk to humans on the phone, but to computers. Maybe that's just my overactive mind, huh? Everywhere I look, I see a phone perched up to an ear. I never knew men liked phones so much. I am saying all of this because we are not repairing the things that needs fixing, yet we are creating more stuff. I read an article about how our students are not performing well on standardized tests. I am not at all surprised. All that's required now is to pass the test and move on; there isn't a lot of hands-on learning any more. Just prepare a PowerPoint and let it do the teaching. . . how does that sound? Don't concern yourself with trying to encourage a student. Or how about the importance of dress? Just accept sagging pants and wearing pajamas to school? Where is the value code? Again, just another different view to ponder. This and more is what I see every day.

Oh, and how did we let Osama bin Laden get away? Our homes have become our prisons; no one is safe; everything that has gone on still goes on.

I just purchased a bookshelf, and I am filling it with books. One day, if my life lasts, I will have a home. Yes, I shared my imaginary home, but I will finish school and buy myself a real home, and die in peace. I have never been on a vacation. I will have one some day. But I can't buy a home working here; I don't have any job security.

I will share this: I am now on another type job, and I can't get the proper training. One person one day, another the next, just get the job done, do what you're told. The person that I once could rely on for fairness is gone to bigger grounds, and the new replacement could not care less. I was having so many problems with one supervisor, and they got so far out of control, that I requested a meeting with him and superiors. On the day of the meeting, I asked if I could record it, but I was told no. Anyway, I have a dated record of the incidents, so I said okay. As I talked, the human resources person's face became red with anger and the new manager didn't know what to think of the many incidents. I felt as if everything was fine, and I was told that he would get back with me on the situations I had brought to his attention. I received a phone call from the Department of Corrections asking what was wrong with me. I thought they meant what had happened, but it was the other way around. Why did I complain about anything? I was told never to do it again, and henceforth, I was to contact them and not the people at the job. Damn, I was under the impression that I was a normal employee, but I was dead wrong. I applied on another job, trying to save my job and get away from this lawless supervisor. The new set of tasks I was told to do was hell. My first day of training was interrupted and I was put back on the bus because the driver was out. This was the first of the year, so I asked the supervisor if someone else could drive the bus, because I needed to learn all those machines. He looked me in my eyes and got in my face and yelled. If he told me to drive, I'd best drive. Did I have a problem with that? My answer was no. In my soul, I did have a problem, but who was I to tell it to? I always reassured myself that I would succeed in school and find a better job, but in reality, I was struggling really badly in school. There was no one to teach a person who came knowing nothing. These were the times I wished that my heart was as before. I would never have remained where I was treated this way. There was a place where I would retreat in times when I felt I was being mistreated and my heart wouldn't allow me to stay. But today is a new day and I do not use that retreat, because I don't want to pay the consequences. So I drive and cry. When you are in my position, you just inhale deeply and go on.

Now back to my training . . . .

Remember back when the fellow told the young boy to deliver the message of murder? Well, his wife no longer works directly with the *people.* She is my trainer now, and her mind is not on training me. So, for what it's worth, as she and the young man text each other all night, I get what training I can. Today she is off, and another person is doing the training. She left , and I am on my own, after twelve hours of pulling and rolling 1500 feet of product, 87 pounds apiece. *I wasn't* told I should have only operated that machine six hours? As I lie down and drift off to sleep, I am awakened by so much pain in my *arm;* it's going numb, all the way down to my hand. It hurts, and I can't go back to sleep.

♦♦♦

The next night, I report this to my supervisor, the same one that I reported it to a while back. He never even reported the complaint. After about two weeks of endless pain, I go to the company doctor and x-rays are taken. Nerve damage is suspected. So I go to the department and seek Worker's Comp, and after going around and around with them, I receive it, so I am placed on light duty. It's constantly being violated, however, and they appear so angry and hostile with me. This *continues* for months and more test are run, and finally it's diagnosed: carpal tunnel syndrome. A date for surgery is set. After surgery, back to light duty. I try to use the hand as much as possible so they don't fire me. My hand is so weak and in pain. It does not matter, for more reasons than one. First, just in case another comes this way and needs a job, I can't risk losing it. I must keep this job. And also, I must prove to myself that I can remain free and productive. It's almost in the middle of summer; I always save my money because you just never know how the cards are stacked. It has been suggested that we take a mini vacation. A vacation . . . now, imagine that! When I was in prison, I would hear some of the women say when they were free they would vacation. I never really thought about it. You can't miss what you've never had . . . right?

♦♦♦

A vacation. Okay. Where? No, first, how much money do we have? That will determine where we go. Okay, I could safely go to Savannah, Georgia. Have you ever been there? I think so, but I also think it does not matter if I have or not. How will we travel? How about renting a car? That's what we did when we took the children back to New York. So we plan a date and make the reservations and excitement is taking over me. I am going on a vacation! As we ride the highways and I see the sights—beautiful fields of flower—pure beauty. Stop and gas up. Back on the road. Love it, simply love it! Stop and get a bite to eat; now this is living. Back on the road, we are almost there. Can't wait. It's dusk . . . dark, and we are coming into the *historical* district . They have a history thick with slavery. Look at the trees. They almost look spooky. It's beautiful the next day, and we go to River Street and then *to* Tybee Island and then to visit *a* museum about the creation of the movie made here. In the Garden of Good and Evil, I think. Let's try this Hampton Inn; it's nice and not far from River Street. The rates are sky high, but it's okay, so we go to the room and get a shower. Do you feel up to walking now? Yes, let's go. The air is sweet and there is plenty to see. I am not used to being out at night anymore, so I am nervous. So this is River Street. It's getting late. Can't visit much. A few shops, so let's come back tomorrow. Back at the motel, I feel like a little action. Hey, you, come here. Let's grab a shower and play some bingo. So we hold each other close and our eyes meet. I can feel the heat. Each touch is a bit much, so temps begin to rise. I explore the beautiful body lying next to me, get myself prepared, and get busy. After about two hours, spent and satisfied, we go to sleep. Get up early the next morning, grab a shower and a bite, and out the door. Back to the museum, and as we sit in the theater and view the history of the town, my mind can't help drifting to slavery and its pain. I cannot picture a large boat with its belly full of humans stacked on top of each other, being taken to be sold as property. Sick, not able to use the toilet or have any privacy, and *maybe lying* next to a dead person *for* three weeks to three months. Being half-fed. . . . Oh, my God, the agony! Going to a place where you can't even speak the language, you can't understand or be understood, to be beaten until your skin *i*s torn like cut meat, and someone rubbing pure salt into the fresh wound to lady ye you. Watching your baby or your wife being raped before your eyes. Seeing your loved one hanging from *a* tree *and* you can't do anything but watch. Picking cotton until *your* hands bleed and better not get the blood on the cotton, picking vegetables from sun up to sun down, no justice nothing for the slave, but a love for each other. The documentary says the masters would put them in boiling hot water if they escaped. It's unbearable just to sit here and listen. But we survived their wrath. I often wonder what we, as a people, have done to deserve God's wrath. But I also am grateful for his mercy. What's this place where we can go on a dinner cruise. I have never been on a cruise before. Let's go. As we board the boat, my excitement is too much. They say there will be live entertainment. Damn, I know who I wish were on this boat . I have a strong imagination; let's see what I come up with. As I sit on this deck, I close my eyes and see over in the far left corner a group of happy people. Let's see who's there. Let's go closer. In one group, I see Ms. Oprah Winfrey *I don't know the words to describe your strength and beauty*, Cicely Tyson *I adore you* , Maya Angelo *your words help make me strong*, George Clooney *with his beautiful eyes*, Brad Pitt *you sexy devil angie broke luck*, and Al Pacino *I like your style sir.*

Also Robert De Niro *my man*, Steven Spielberg *I like your humanness*, Richard Gere *you are simply the best*, Anthony *Hopkins you are one smart man, Ellen DeGeneresi bet you are a nice person* Oh, my! Look this way please. Now feast your eyes on this: having a laugh are Terrance Howard *you are so down to earth*, Denzel Washington *your wife must be the luckiest lady* , and Tyler Perry with his pretty kiss-able-looking lips. And Mr. Michael Jackson—he is so mysterious *and mike you are the one to make it happen*. Look, there is Tom Joyner *for ever talking yak* and his staff. And Tupac *the rose in the concrete tells it's on story* and Sean Combs *keep on keeping on p diddy* ! The ladies with them compliment their swag. Michael Bolton *you will never know the comforts your songs brought on my many runs around the prison yard* and T Pain *I lke your energy*, Li'l Wayne *you are to cute*, Chris Brown *you dance like mj*, T*I keep it real as always*. I wonder why Whitney is without Bobby.*probaly better off* Everyone is having a great time laughing and talking drinking as the music plays on the upper deck. I see the Rev. Dr. Martin Luther King J *sir I held on to your words* r., and Malcolm X. Sure is good to have them aboard. I can remember back when I was a child. Dr. King . . . that look in his eyes when he came around to the room and on the porch. His words *life* would get better by and by; I did not understand that then, but I sure do now. Chaplain Susan Bishop and my best friend Maultie and her crew*, and her favorite reverend Milner* Bishop Dale Bronner and the first lady. I see my favorite pastor, Rev. Frank Salter and the first lady, and Bishop TD Jake*s, there is Bishop Eddie Long lady ys favorite. Oh my there is Bill Glass world of champions and I love you Karois hey chap kabeer always real, A.J. Sabree* It's such a lovely crowd! Hey, I almost missed her— Angelina Jolie with her fine self. Now tell me, isn't this a nice crew? Each person named has inspired my life in a special way.

No, I did not name everyone. I named them because every person needs a hero and they are a few of mine. It would take a lifetime for me to list them all. As the music begins to play, a waiter asks me what I would like to drink. Now I am back to reality, but this is fantastic. I see the fish jump out the water. It's blissful and peaceful . . . . Oh, so nice. This is great, just great. Now back on shore, we travel River Street and listen to the tune of a trumpet player. It's almost like being in a storybook, and my favorite stars are here, like the cast from Lord of the Rings. I am happy. It is the time now to go to Tybee Island. I look forward to getting there and taking pictures. Oh, my! Look at the beautiful waves, children running and screaming and playing, walking in the sand, jogging and looking for shells along the way. Go to the concession stand, get something to drink, and let's get in that water. Now this is nice—real nice. After splashing water on each other and having the time of my life, it's time to go, and a heaviness is around my shoulders for a day or two. I was free, and now I must return to my reality, and I pray to survive it. I have a church to visit. I think the group is trying to get a home for the women. This is very important. See, it is easy for people who have never been in prison to not understand how hard it is, so they have come up with these boards of directors. They don't want our input as to the housing structure and how we will go about selecting the women, so now I must insist, because we don't have a lot of room for mistakes. And yes, we would offer good insight and needed input. We are going around and around with this. The women who volunteer are so nice, but they are only seen when we have a meeting, and no one returns calls or follows up on what they promise. But once a year, we get together. I don't know if I like that much, but I have recruited another dedicated sister, and I know that she is down for this cause, so let's move forward. Okay, that fell through; there will be no house, so what is the purpose of this group? Just to meet and promise? This is not what I had in mind. There is a great need for a transitional house that has structure and will give the women being released a ray of hope, but how can this help. . . just meeting and talking and no action. Now the members are losing heart. We need each other. I would love to open a place for the women where they wouldn't be pressured about money until they could find work. And I'd like to start them an account, to have something to live off. But I must continue to try to find someone to help me help them.

♦♦♦

The year is coming to an end and there is rumor of a recession. The price of gas is sky high, over three dollars a gallon. How did this happen ? I mean I can feel the pressure at my job. The unemployment rate is rising high. What's this? Damn, Mike! They are taking Michael Jackson back to court, and he looks so weary. I just don't believe what they are saying about him. I feel sorry for him. Hs mother is right by his side. These phony-ass people! When he was popular, they loved him. Now, they are dragging him through the mud, and they don't want to even hear his name. They are forever fucking with that man.

Now what's with the men wearing their pants so big? They call it sagging. What's the point? Dealer's choice I guess. Times are changing, big time, everywhere. I have written a play for seniors coming out of school. I have not saved enough yet to have it produced, but I will. I tried to cover different subjects of importance. Sometimes we are so caught up in the hype we miss things, and they usually are important.

Back to this recession . . .

Here at my job I know my ass will be out the door because they see about their own and I am not one of them. I wish that they had been straight up with me. This school has taken its toll. I can't get any help, and I need this so bad, so I will just hold on the best I can. I know that timing is everything. I have had my transcript sent. They see that I can learn. Damn. They act as if they feel sorry for me. Now, that grips my ass. Don't feel sorry; teach me. I don't invest this much time and energy for sympathy. I get off work after twelve hours and stay after class, going to the library, staying there until I can't keep my eyes open any longer. What else can I do? Looking outside, I see that a storm is brewing . They say we have global warming. I will study that some so that I can get the full meaning. This is election year, and I am waiting to see who will run and how that works. I don't have a lot of faith in politics . . . never even voted. Hell, most of the time . . . well, I will refrain from that comment. Every day I ride my bike to and from work. I do that for time and peace of mind and for exercise. I have this overwhelming feeling of pressure. Workplace situations are quite trying. I have learned to pray a lot as I ride. I look at how people keep their property and how we can get so complacent, we stop growing. Does life lose its glamour? What happens when we just add more stuff to the carport or become so systematic do we lose our drive. Look at how this yard is kept; the grass is overgrown and it causes this pretty home to be not so pretty. Now, as I ride further, I look at this place—it's well kept, with flowers, neatly organized. Everything is well kept. I was watching this movie last night and I saw where just as we keep our homes, we keep each other. This man was so into his work, he forgot his wife's needs. It seems to me that life is an ongoing job until we die.

I know that I jump from one subject to the other. Just try to keep up; that's how I think. You should know that by now.

I had a few tests run. One was this: they put me somewhat to sleep, but I could see what they were doing. I felt something inside of me. It was a camera and I saw on this TV a picture of my insides. It was very pink. The test was to see if I had cancer. Why am I talking about this? Well, the reason is we shouldn't wait to be dying to start trying to live. I thought as they told me I needed the test, hell, I have never lived, *and* now we are checking on dying. Innocence and time can never be replaced. I have been robbed of one, and the other is going fast.

♦♦♦

Let's move on now. What's this I hear on the news? An African American and a woman are running for president. What? No way! Come on, stop playing. Now that's something to talk about.

Let's talk about the female. Her name is Hilary Clinton. I have always liked her style. She is very intelligent. I like strong women, like Harriet Tubman. I could never hear enough about her strength. And there have been countless others. How in the world did this happen? Women are farther back on the slates than slaves. I believe that the world still doesn't want us where we should be, but we are strong, and we persevere. Here is another interesting subject: Ms. O is backing this gentleman. I like her. Now the race is on. Here at my job there are some nasty comments being made. They think this is a joke, and everyone is laughing, but I wouldn't expect anything else from them. Check this out: this man doesn't ever speak, and now he asks me who am I going to vote for. Not only did I say I would vote for this African American, but I will run with him as I much as I can. He said that I was just throwing my vote away. I would rather throw it away than do nothing. I must pay him attention and see what his chances are. I like his wife—a tower of strength. Now look at the tactics. Look at America, and listen to the venom and tell me the sore of racism is healed. Like hell it is! I really don't know what to think, but I do know what I am going to do—I will stand 100% behind him—win, lose, or draw.

They found Michel Jackson not guilty. I was at the Varsity and this news reporter asked me if I felt that he was guilty. Really, in my heart of hearts, I feel that he is innocent, yet eccentric. Look at Mike—he looks so tired! I wonder if he is healthy?

Now back to this race. Hilary is swinging low blows, and it's looking shaky as hell, but I will go over to the campsite in this town and do my part. Joyner is helping. Why doesn't everyone just pitch in? The blacks, I mean. What is this preacher talking about? He's wrong for that approach. I am glad the candidate is severing ties with this preacher. Oh, it's looking better every day. I go from door to door. Some people are kind, but the majority are not. Doesn't matter. I bought this tee shirt that says "he's black and I am proud." Boy, do I get the looks. I don't care. I am going to wear it anyway. Since when do I give a rat's ass what people say?

Now Hilary, I am starting to think things about your so-called loyalty to blacks. Not good. I have never been so involved in this political mess, but I am in for the long haul. He is so young, and I do see hope. He has a different approach: he'll look at the shape we Americans are in, gas sky-high, people losing their homes, no jobs, the crime rate climbing, big companies going belly-up. We need change. What harm can he do that's not already done?

Now, why did these people at this job ever let felons work here? They never intended to do right by us. Now they are pulling my piss every other day. It's embarrassing to have to be led into this clinic all the time. What the fuck!

Now look at this other man. He is kind of old. I think that doesn't make him unable, but it's how he talks that causes concern in me.

I like him for several reasons, this Democratic candidate. Now they are giving his wife the blues over a statement that she made about loving America. I like this picture—his wife and his kids, how he is so comfortable with his family. This is a busy election, and it's more than just a race; everyone is slinging boulders. But he's not. I wonder. He definitely knows what to say, and I believe that if he is elected, he can back it up with action. Who will his vice presidential partner be if he receives the nod? Everyone's talking. I mean even in Africa, and they are placing bets. I have lived in this world long enough to know there is nothing wrong with failing if you give it a strong try. That's what I am talking about. Look my man Robert De Niro. He is on his side, and there is Ted Kennedy. That has to stand for something. And I believe Mr. Spielberg is also, but I could be wrong. What's this? Jessie Jackson cut his nuts off! What's wrong with you, colored man. I can't say that I don't fear for his life, because I do. I think back to Malcolm X and how the nation had him assassinated. That broke my heart. I liked his fiery spirit. But as I think back, I should not fear for his life. I loved Mr. King, and he died a bad death. Why is it so wrong for the blacks to get ahead and be recognized as being more than slaves? From what I've read, we were a proud, productive people. Why, God, why? Why and when? Only God has those answers. I will make a few more calls. I asked a few blacks if they will vote for him, and I did not like their answers. Like, "What for? The decision is already made." Damn, the only way I ever received anything different is that I had to do something different. Like I want a house and I want to be able to keep it. I can't bank on my present job, but I can get an education and better my chances of employment. I tried to call my children, but I couldn't. That hurt so bad. But what can I do? I can't believe that it's this way. I want to help troubled youth. They are our tomorrow. I tried to contact Mr. Tyler Perry with an idea. But small people don't matter, and I could never get in touch with him. I tried also Ms. Winfrey, but there again, no. Why don't they listen to poor people? Don't we have something to say? That's one of the many reasons I like this candidate. He listens to poor people. I look at this situation—why do people pretend to care? Maybe because it is convenient to do so, for their own gain. I am hungry for the truth in life.

♦♦♦

May I return to the beginning for a brief moment? Remember I mentioned a sister early on? My older sister, the first. Well, I found her, and the reunion was sad. I called her, and on one occasion we had dinner. She drank plenty of wine and her truth began to roll out of her mouth. You would never imagine this was the fine lady of a few minutes before. She cried and allowed the demons of her past out, and it was like looking at the devil himself. The blocked pain of her childhood and the bitterness of being given away by her mother, who then kept the other children that she birthed. I tried to tell her she got the better deal; we all fell amongst the ruins. She didn't hear me. As time went on, I tried to reach out and be her sister, but she doesn't want that now.

One day, I called, and she just told me that we weren't raised together; we just had the same mother. Her words cut like a knife. She was telling me, in other words, don't keep calling me. I don't want to be anything more to you. The family I have is cruel and unforgiving and in pain. I mention this because as I look at the candidate and his family, I see the greatest gift of all: a united family. There can be no greater joy, can there? I am learning that perhaps I should move on and just forget family. How does one continue to reach out when no one is extending a hand in return? It cuts like a giant knife not to have the support of family. That's one of the many reasons I joined the prison ministry: they are my family; they accept me, and I them.

Today there are problems with gang violence. Now, I have been in a gang, as a youth, and my reason for joining was that it was a place of acceptance. Abused people seek power because they don't feel very powerful. When ghetto youth experience the feeling of being unloved and misunderstood, it is a bad combination. I later discovered that just as the adults had taken advantage of me and my parents didn't love me, neither did those of my fellow gang members. We were a group of confused, hurt, angry youth, and the truth escaped us. After so many near-fatal blows, I come now to a truce of hope. I am learning that I must first love myself before anyone else can love me, and if I don't stand for something, I will fall for anything. This man, the candidate, is a fighter and a ray of hope. I never mentioned this, I don't think, but being black has been very painful, and the obstacles are vast. The scales have always been unbalanced, and a difference is always there, even to this day. Why, I ask, does it have to be this way? No, even if this man wins, it probably will not erase the color line. I used to say they took the shackles off our feet and put them on our minds. Today it's a different type of slavery—a stronger brand. It appears that we have made it, but look deeper and see the invisible limitations. Everyone has tightened their game; it's mental all the way. I once saw in a movie where a man asked another man how you catch a monkey. The answer was, with something shiny. Tell me, who is the monkey and what's being dangled that's shiny? I see so much progress in my people, yet I see our youth being forgotten. They are our tomorrow; we must take a better look at them. I think of all this when I look into his happy, dancing eyes. Yes, I will stand with you, sir. Yes, I will. I see others feel the same way. Can we win? Hell, yes, we can! Before they let a woman have the presidency, they will give it to him. Then there is this other fellow. I don't know.

There was once a time when blacks had nothing but each other, and we stood strong. Maybe we should try that again, especially now. People are saying that the world will end if he wins. The last time I read the Bible, it said that the day and time wasn't known. Now, his wife is strong and has a straight back. I trust her words. Just look in her bright eyes. I think they thought he was playing, but he is dead serious, and I am also. I began the journey to call and visit homes. I am not doing so well down here, so I will try another area where the people are not so color-conscious. This, I must say, is very stimulating for me. Since I have been out of prison, I have done everything that was required of me to be a law-abiding citizen. Imagine me, the outlaw, a law abiding citizen and a productive member of this human society. That's what I am talking about.

♦♦♦

Today I went with my brother to church. I have never done that before. To rob a joint maybe, but never to church. I had a wonderful time. The singing was excellent, and I sat by this lady and she emanated love. I had such a wonderful time! I was invited by the head of the prison ministry, and I invited him over after the service. Do you remember back a few pages I said when I was a child I was raised on Mitchell Street? Well, that's where the church is, and in the same exact spot as when I was a child. After the service, I asked him if he would go with me back to our childhood neighborhood and pray with me that God will lift that long, heavy burden from our hearts and minds. So we did.

I tell you, I really don't know what is happening in this world. Now don't get me wrong, and let's not get the message twisted. I am no saint by any means, but I do have enough sense to know that with all that's going on in this world, the only way we will get it right is to unite and cry out as one.

This is the hottest debate ever, and my friend is holding his own, with the help of us people. I believe that he will run on, and we'll see what the end will be. The hounds of hell are out and about, and everyone is holding their breath and guns to see if this black man wins. The female runner is strong and long-winded. The other gent is strong also. It's time to select running mates. Let's see who they will be. Oh, we must see who receives the nod, who will run the real race. The other gent received the nod for rep. Now, a run of death between my man and the female. Mud is being slung, tempers are flaring, and the race is on. She's drinking and swearing and my man is pacing. Let's see what happens. I believe my man will get the nod, but let's just make a few more calls and canvas a little more. I like how the churches are trying to lift a toe to help. Okay, the race is close. I am talking about very, very close, between him and the female, and she has her husband in her corner, and he was once the man himself. Up mountains, into very deep valleys, my man is non- relenting, and I see stamina,, hope, and perseverance in action.

Damn, what's this? This football player is getting ready to take a fall for dog fighting. What the hell! What is hunting? See, that's what I am talking about. If one person does something that's wrong, it's given a more appropriate name, but if another does something similar, it's given a name that will involve the prison system. Now that's exactly what I was speaking about when I said earlier that the slavery mentality has been rearranged, but is in full force. I cannot believe that the people are going to end this man's future over this. It's all right to go out at dawn and brutally kill the mother or father deer for sport, or go and shoot the beautiful duck from the sky, or put a chicken on a machine that causes it to continually bleed, or skin the hide off of an animal for a beautiful coat for someone who already owns uncounted coats. My take on this is that it's wrong to mistreat anyone or anything for any reason.

Back to the race . . .

Well, it's almost over—all the debates, all the promises. The whole world is looking, and the fever is high. I need him to win. Why? This may or may not make sense, but I am very sensitive to my people's plight, and I just know in my heart that we, as a people, were not a mistake here in this world, and we are not bad, as the world has painted us. We have importance and great significance. I think back to history. I have always wanted the spilled blood of yesterday to be avenged. I need to see us on top before I die. Give him a chance; let's see what he does. I remember as a child as I saw Dr. Mr. Martin L. King, Jr., and I remember the look in his eyes as he looked at us children and said, "By and by it will get better." I need that to come true, so that even with the life I have lived, there is hope of change, and in the future, we will strive for better and achieve it.

I read a story about this girl who had been abducted at age eleven, and eighteen years later, she resurfaced. All that time she had been held captive, a slave to this old man who molested her, and she bore two children from him. My God, can we for just a moment talk about how she must have felt after so long? The authorities stopped looking for her, and she was left to this monster. I remember the filth and the pain and just how ashamed I felt when my youth was taken. Webster's doesn't have the words sufficient to express the pain. If I were an artist, I couldn't draw the picture. She was such a pretty little girl, and innocent. They say the children have never been to a doctor. Damn the human race. How far will we go in our sickness? There is so much in my mind and heart I will never understand .

The nomination is fast approaching and the numbers are looking good. I will walk for you, sir, and I will continue to place calls. America needs change; we really do. I must not be the only one to feel this way. Look at the voter turnout. It's here, and my nerves are jumping. I must go to work, so I can't see it. Damn!

It's the morning after, and we made it! Can you believe it? We made it! Now the task begins. Oh, my God, we made it. I just think back to one day when I was at the aquarium in Atlanta, and I had on that tee shirt on that says, "he's black and I am proud," and how people just stared as if I was the last fool on this earth. Like how can a black man win? Ah, ha! He was nominated to run for the dems. Now isn't that something? Maybe now everyone will join in and help. The race is on, and look . . . they say he doesn't have sense enough to come out of the rain. It is raining, and he is making a speech. Now, the spirit I knew we had is coming out, not just in African Americans but anyone and everyone who wants change. So much excitement is in the air, so much hope for a better day. Everywhere I go, everyone is talking. We made history the right way, and we are headed for the election. God be with us, please. It's here. America has its first African American president! Congratulations, America! Come on, let's celebrate, let's dance, let's sing, let's rebuild what has been torn down, let's make a place for everyone, not just the haves, but also the have nots, and anyone who wishes to make this world a better place. This will not come easy, because America is struggling to stay afloat. Maybe we took too much for granted. Maybe we got too greedy. Maybe we just turned our heads the other way. I have renewed hopes for tomorrow. I will do my part to rebuild and reconstruct tomorrow. Yes, even I, the once lawless outlaw now have a vision of hope. I had lunch with my niece, and as we ate, we talked about how good the food was. We both are trying to fit in a world that is not very sensitive to hurt, offended persons such as my niece and me. She has never accepted herself. She told me that her youth was filled with memories of pain, of rejection, of partiality. Someone was favored over her, and she was angry. That anger spilled into her tomorrows, and I mentioned this because I saw this very same thing happen in my own youth, and it hurt to be rejected. But what hurts even more is when you are not able to tell the person who rejects you of the pain, and they can't tell you their side, and it has a snowball effect. Rejection has the same effect as shame. When you learn to live with it, it governs your life. Everything I do reflects my pain—even my joy. Don't try to understand; hell, I can't even do that. I told a member that I was writing this book, and he said, "What the hell are you doing that for?

You are not famous. Who would read it?" I said, "I don't know." Well, it's like this: the election, to me, was payment for the many generations of pain we have suffered. It was not in vain. The same with this book. I write it so that my pathetic life will not have been in vain. I hope that any of the contents can and will be used by those in need of hope.

I have only a couple of true friends, and I mentioned one in particular. Her name is Maultie. She is the best. When I told her of this project, as with any other idea I've ever had, she stood right by my side. Being friends with her comes easy. I know that she has my back. She wasn't always just my best friend; she was my lover, and even in that, she was great. I trust her, and that's saying so much. As I watch her, busy with her endeavors, I think what a selfless person she is. She's bold and intelligent, not to mention very beautiful. I love you, Maultie.

Oh my God, this is sad news! My favorite entertainer has just been pronounced dead. Oh, no, not Michael Jackson! God, please let it be a mistake, please. It's true. No matter what was said of him, he was my Michael. So happy about one man and devastated by the other news. Rest in peace, MJ. I am happy to see that whereas just months ago there was hate for him, now, as I look at this memorial service, they are trying to show some kind of love. Well, at least some respect for his contributions. I think of him as he used to be when I was a girl and he was just a boy. I was so proud of him, and the feeling only grew over time. Can you really imagine being a child exposed to as much as he was? I mean, he didn't have any childhood, any time to grow as a normal boy would. You know, I mention that because I understand what the loss of a childhood means to a person. Someone who has never really lost something of value will never understand the giant hole in one's soul for that which has been lost. We live in a world that needs to learn to believe again and trust again and love and forgive again, so that we can create a better place to leave behind. I look at Ms. Oprah Winfrey as she reaches out to help. I have watched her on several occasions, and she doesn't give me the impression of a pretending woman, but of one who uses her influence to make it happen. I don't know how it happened . . . you know, like what caused it, but I do know that the world has gained some trust in her, just as I did many years ago. I was so happy when she stood behind my man. Many prayers for that.

I started this writing in 1993, and it is now 2009. As I ride my bike different places and I look into the beautiful sky, my mind allows me to create a world that is different—kind and caring. No, my life isn't a rose garden and never will be. The thorns are tall and very sharp, and every day I face my demons. With this attitude, it's not what I am confronted with, but how I handle the confrontation, and no, I cannot run from fear, but

I stand before it and continue to move on. No, I don't win every battle. Ever since I have been free, I have been, and still am, challenged every day, just as everyone else is. But I go on. And actually, my life is incomplete. I have never regained a relationship with my children. In fact, when I was denied participation in my son's graduation, I thought that I would die. Some part of me did die. Every time I must look the other way on the job, I manage to go on. Sometimes the story just doesn't have a happy ending, but you must go on.

Come inside my heart and my soul. Let's walk down the aisles of disaster. We've done that. Let's go to prison. We've done that, too. Let's go now to mistrust, abuse, pain, and misunderstanding. You must know that the road of life may never be easy. You may never find love, but you must believe in change and a better tomorrow. You must find a way to believe in yourself, learn to love yourself, and be who you are. We cannot change yesterday, only learn from it and continue on.

This is to my beloved sisters and my beloved brothers the words to this song fit my thoughts perfectly how do we learn to say good bye to yesterday, to what we never had ,but to the good times if any that made us laugh we will always have each other I don't know where this road will lead all I know is where we've been ,and what we have been through we survived only through GODs grace and mercy if we see tomorrow , I hope that its worth all the pain I'll take with me the memories to be my sunshine after the rain, I love each one of you with all my heart as I know that you love me.

To my beloved parents I tried to find any and all answers that would justify, but there is none, but I did discover this in order for me to live I must forgive both of you for everything and I do.

To the entire children mine and theirs find a way to forgive us of our short comings that way you will be forgiven for yours.

To my beautiful friend Sharon I have never known a more selfless person with my heart I love you.

To maultie thanks for always keeping it real with me I love you always.

A special thank you to the department of corrections there is a saying prison will make you or break you, congratulations you did both.

To the staff at prison when I served time I know at times it was hard to care but you always did, not all but you know who you are.

There were times of true despair I just needed a kind ear a forgiving heart someone to listen every prison ministry that came and shared their time and love to the forgotten ones may GOD add a special measure to your life.

From the depths of my soul this is to the many people I have harmed physically and mentally I don't have the eloquence that would express the depths of my sorrow, try to find a way to forgive Eloise I love you and I do forgive you.

Life is good today until the next time.

The End.